LARGE PRINT RECIPES FOR A HEALTHY LIFE

Low Cholesterol, Low Fat, Low Sodium, No Added Sugar

by Judith Caditz, Ph.D.

The Center for the Partially Sighted
Los Angeles, California

To Allan, Michael and David and your continuing good health. Your appreciation of low fat foods without added sugar or artificial ingredients has been an inspiration to me.

CONTENTS

CHAPTER 3—DRESSINGS AND SAUCES   49

DRESSINGS

SAUCES

CHAPTER 6— MUFFINS, QUICK BREADS, CRACKERS AND YEAST BREADS   165

MUFFINS

QUICK BREADS

YEAST BREADS AND CRACKERS

CREPES

CEREALS

PANCAKES

LIST OF LOW VISION TIPS

APPENDIX 245

Tables:

FOREWARD

Many people who experience a significant loss of eyesight become very discouraged about their cooking ability or they become fearful of accidents in the kitchen. They feel their dietary choices are extremely limited and no longer within their control, although they know they would benefit from a healthier diet.

Others become more interested in a healthy diet as they get older. Unfortunately, that's also when the vision system starts to change. For most of us, it's a simple matter of holding material farther away until our arms become too short and we need reading glasses (or large print). However, for millions of visually impaired people in this country, glasses no longer give enough help and special magnifying devices are needed.

This cookbook was prepared for people who need a little extra help to maintain a healthy diet and regain a sense of confidence in the kitchen. The recipes have all been selected and tested by the author, Judith Caditz, Ph.D., who knows first-hand the role of nutrition in maintaining good health. Because of her own reduced vision, she is eager to share her knowledge with others who have trouble reading recipes from regular print cookbooks.

Another unique feature of <u>Large Print Recipes for a Healthy Life</u> is the target of the proceeds. All income received from the sale of this cookbook will go directly to support the Diabetes and Vision Loss Program at The Center for the Partially Sighted. This program helps individuals improve blood sugar control through low vision optometric care, behavior modification, psychological support, vision rehabilitation techniques and adaptive aids.

For more information about these groups, please contact: Dr. Pam Thompson at 310-458-3501.

LaDonna S. Ringering, Ph.D. President/CEO The Center for the Partially Sighted.

FOREWARD

Judith Caditz has taken her personal and professional commitment to good health and her delight in cooking and has put together a wonderful collection of over 100 nutritious, diet-conscious large print recipes for a healthy life.

Each recipe has been carefully adjusted to be low in fat, cholesterol, sodium and sugar, yet great in taste. It will be helpful to you that the nutritional analysis includes calories, protein, fat, carbohydrate, fiber, cholesterol and sodium. Diabetes exchanges are listed for those who need this information. Whether you're watching your diet or simply want to eat healthier, this is the cookbook you've been looking for.

As a consulting nutritionist and registered dietitian, I commend Judith for her efforts and I wholeheartedly recommend her book to everyone who loves to cook and eat the healthy way.

Bon Appetit!

Joyce N. Carlson, R.D
Consulting Nutritionist
in Private Practice
Santa Monica,
Cafifornia

ACKNOWLEDGMENTS

I wish to express my appreciation to the people who helped make this book possible. I thank the committee members for their support: Joyce Carlson, R.D., Gerald A. Levine, M.D., La-Donna S. Ringering, Ph.D., and Alan L. Shabo, M.D. I thank the organizations and individuals who sponsored this work: MetLife, Arrowhead Mills, Com-putrition, Gita Rosenwald and Howard Schiller. Ani Chakmakian and the staff at Computrition worked on the dietary analysis and diabetes exchanges. Gita Rosenwald of Graphiti, Ink carefully designed the format of the book with her desktop publishing skills. Pat Jordan is of ongoing assistance in marketing of the book. Howard Schiller created the cover designs. Elda Zeldis conferred with me on low vision tips. Bob Baker Repro-graphics produced the covers.

I thank Allan M. Caditz, J.D. for his continuing encouragement, patience and support in making every aspect of this book possible.

Judith Caditz, Ph.D.
The Center for the Partially Sighted
Los Angeles, CA 90025
March, 1992

Also by Judith Caditz

Diabetes, Visual Impairment, and Group Support: A Guidebook, 1988

The Center for the Partially Sighted
Los Angeles, California 90025

INTRODUCTION

My interest in creating these recipes and writing this book stems from several life experiences. I grew up in a home where eating fresh vegetables, whole grains, and fresh fruits was the major theme. It has been perfectly natural for me to use whole wheat flour, brown rice and lean protein foods. Also, we usually raised our own vegetables and fruits without the use of pesticides. There were exceptions to this healthful way of eating. At times we ate more fat and whole eggs, especially on the holidays.

In my work here, I have adapted many holiday foods to be consistent with a low fat, low sodium diet. Some of the recipes are modifications of my mother's specialties, which were in turn recipes she adapted from her mother.

During the past seventeen years, I have been instrumental in developing the Diabetes Education/Support Group at The Center for the Partially Sighted in Los Angeles, California. I have been the leader in many of the groups. One of the major tasks I have undertaken is to inform group participants of the importance of following certain dietary guidelines—low fat, low cholesterol, low sodium, and no added sugar. I have followed these guidelines myself during the thirty three years that I have worked at controlling my own diabetes. I am firmly convinced that it improves one's quality of life to be successful (at least most of the time) in taking command of this major area of life— eating according to the best scientific information at this time. There is so much we can not control, whether it be trying to attain perfect blood sugars, blood pressure, or health in general. The factors we *can* control make us not only feel better physically, but also emotionally because we feel we are trying our best to steer the ship.

During these years working with my patients in the support groups and with myself, I became convinced that what is good for people with diabetes is good for everyone. Until future scientific evidence may change our thinking, it is hard to argue with staying on a low cholesterol and low fat diet with emphasis placed on complex carbohydrates, vegetables, whole grains, legumes and fruits.

In addition to controlling what we eat, I feel it is essential for us to try to exercise as much as possible within our physical limitations.

However, before embarking on any major changes in your meal plan or your exercise regimen, I suggest you discuss these ideas with your physician.

DIETARY GUIDELINES

The following analysis is based on information from the American Cancer Society, the American Diabetes Association, the American Heart Association, the National Academy of Sciences and the Surgeon General's Report.

Limit Consumption of Fat and Cholesterol.

The main organizations studying diet and nutrition are in basic agreement about the types of foods we should consume. Today, there is great emphasis on the reduction of fats, particularly saturated fats and on the reduction of cholesterol. Tables 1 and 2 in the Appendix will guide you in determining the cholesterol and fatty acid content of foods.

The National Academy of Sciences, in a multidisciplinary perspective, summarizes some of the major findings (2). The statement on fat consumption is as follows:

"Reduce total fat intake to 30% or less of calories. Reduce saturated fatty acid intake to less than 10% of calories, and the intake of cholesterol to less than 300 mg. (milligrams) daily. The intake of fat and cholesterol can be reduced by substituting fish, poultry without skin, and low or non-fat dairy products for fatty meats and whole-milk dairy products; by choosing more vegetables, fruits, cereals, and legumes; and by limiting oils, fats, egg yolks, and fried or other fatty foods." (National Academy of Sciences, p. 11).

The American Diabetes Association and the American Heart Association are in agreement with the idea that it is best to limit fat intake to less than 30% of daily calories (3,4). The National Academy of Sciences states that it is prudent to eat even less than this amount and substitute vegetables, complex carbohydrates and fruits for fat. Further, it recommends that only 10% of fat intake should be saturated. The American Cancer Society similarly advises us to reduce fat consumption (5). The Surgeon General concurs and suggests that we use little or no fat in food preparation (6). The National Academy of Sciences states there is much evidence that a diet low in cholesterol and fat reduces the risk of atherosclerotic cardiovascular diseases. Further, there is evidence that a high fat diet is associated with the development of some types of cancer, such as breast, prostate, and colon cancers (2).

It is important for all of us to take these recommendations seriously and to avoid foods with high fat content. It is particularly wise to avoid saturated fats which are contained in animal products, as well as in coconut, palm and palm kernel oils. I try to keep the percentage of calories from fat down to 10% each day.

Limit Sodium Consumption.

The American Heart Association suggests that we eat less than 3 grams (3000 milligrams) of sodium per day (4). The American Diabetes Association recommends even less—between 1 and 3 grams per day (3). Less than 1/2 teaspoon of salt is close to this amount. Sodium is naturally occurring in some foods, so it is best to add very little salt in cooking. The National Academy of Sciences states we should use very little salt in cooking and avoid using the salt shaker at the table. Avoid highly processed foods, salt preserved foods and pickled foods (2). The American Cancer

Society further advises us to avoid salt-cured, nitrite-cured and smoked foods which may be related to the development of cancers of the stomach and esophagus (5). Refer to Table 3 in the Appendix for a list of the sodium content of foods.

The Surgeon General reports that among Americans the average sodium intake per day is 4 to 6 grams (4000 to 6000 milligrams) (6). This is much higher than any of the major organizations studied here recommend.

Many studies report a link between high salt intake and the development of hypertension. Those prone to hypertension can help control their blood pressure by following a diet limited in sodium. In addition, there is some evidence that highly salted and pickled foods may be associated with the formation of stomach cancer.

Consume A Large Percentage of Complex Carbohydrates and Fiber.

The American Diabetes Association advises us to consume 55%-60% of our daily calories in the form of complex carbohydrates, which include cereals, grains, vegetables, legumes and fruits (3). Complex carbohydrates contain soluble fiber, such as those in oat bran, beans, and insoluble fibers, such as those in wheat bran. The ADA also recommends that we eat as much as 40 grams of fiber per day. The American Cancer Society and the Surgeon General also recommend eating plenty of high fiber foods (5,6). Table 4 in the Appendix contains the fiber content of many foods.

The National Academy of Sciences helps us decide what to eat by stating the following:

"Every day eat five or more servings of a combination of vegetables and fruits, especially green and yellow vegetables and citrus fruits. Also, increase intake of starches and other complex carbohydrates by eating six or more daily servings of a combination of breads, cereals, and legumes."(National Academy of Sciences, p. 13). One serving is equivalent to the amounts specified in the diabetes exchanges discussed in the next section.

The American Cancer Society recommends that we eat more cabbage family vegetables (5). These include broccoli, cauliflower, brussels sprouts, all types of cabbages, and kale. These protect us against cancer of the colon and rectum, stomach, and respiratory system. The Society also recommends eating foods with beta-carotene, such as carrots, peaches, apricots, squash and broccoli. There is evidence that beta-carotene protects us against cancers of the esophagus, larynx, and lungs. Also, eat plenty of foods rich in Vitamin C, such as citrus fruits, cantaloupe, strawberries, red and green peppers, broccoli, and tomatoes.

Reduce Protein Intake from the Customary Amount in the American Diet.

High protein diets often contain too much fat, especially saturated fat. Further, in people with the potential for kidney disease, eating too much protein taxes the kidneys. In addition, as people grow older, their kidney function declines, so reducing protein intake is a prudent idea.

The recommended daily amount of protein is 0.8 grams per kilogram of body weight (2,3). This is about 43 grams for a person weighing 120 pounds, 54 grams for a person weighing 150 pounds and 65 grams for a person weighing 180 pounds. The National Academy of Sciences suggests that we can eat up to twice that amount (2). However, there is growing evidence that people with diabetes can preserve their kidney function by being on a low protein diet. Table 5 in the Appendix contains a list of foods with their protein content. Table 6 in the Appendix shows the phosphorous content of some foods, since some people must also watch their daily intake of phosphorous in order to preserve kidney function. It is advisable for you to discuss a low protein diet with your physician before placing yourself on such a plan.

For those on low protein diets, please note that some foods, such as beans, nuts, seeds and chicken soup (which is free on the Diabetes Exchanges) contain significant amounts of protein. Remember that low protein does not mean no protein.

Limit Intake of Sugar.

Refined sugar provides "empty" calories, without essential vitamins and minerals. Sugars also cause tooth decay. The Surgeon General reminds us that the presence of simple sugars causes plaque to form on the teeth (6).

One's customary diet is best maintained by avoiding refined sugars and not adding them to cooking. However, please note that the person with diabetes, especially insulin dependent diabetes (Type I diabetes), may occasionally require dextrose or another simple sugar in order to raise the blood sugar if it falls too low.

READING LABELS

In order to best follow the dietary guidelines suggested here, it is a good idea for you to know how to determine the percentage of carbohydrate, protein and fat calories in packaged foods. Carbohydrate and protein contain 4 calories for every gram. Fat contains 9 calories for every gram.

Calculating the Percentage of Carbohydrate, Protein, and Fat.

It is possible for you to figure out which foods are the best choices. Let us analyze a few examples:

Sardines, 3 ounces canned

Calories: 230

Protein: 16 grams X 4 = 64 calories

Carbohydrate: 1 gram X 4 = 4 calories

Fat: 18 grams X 9 = 162 calories

Sodium: 400 milligrams (there are sodium reduced sardines containing 120 milligrams for 3 ounces)

28% of total calories are from protein

2% of total calories are from carbohydrate

70% of total calories are from fat

This product is high in fat content. You might be able to eat a small portion (1 ounce) in a meal with plenty of complex carbohydrates and vegetables. Your total daily fat should be considered to see if you are out of line.

❦

Halibut, 3-1/2 ounces raw

Calories: 95

Protein: 21 grams X 4 = 84 calories

Carbohydrate: 0.0 grams = 0 calories

Fat: 1.2 grams X 9 = 11 calories

Sodium: 54 milligrams

88% of total calories are from protein

0% of calories are from carbohydrate

12% of total calories are from fat

Halibut has a significantly lower amount of fat than sardines and is a better choice as a protein food.

❦

Whole Wheat Pasta (no eggs) 2 ounces (uncooked)

Calories: 210

Protein: 8.2 X 4 = 32.8 calories

Carbohydrate: 42.5 X 4 = 170 calories

Fat: 0.8 X 9 = 7.2 calories

Sodium: less than 10 milligrams

16% of total calories are from protein

81% of total calories are from carbohydrate

3% of total calories are from fat

Since the fat content is low and there is a large proportion of complex carbohydrate, this is a good choice as a starch.

Potato Chips, 1 ounce

Calories: 150

Protein: 0.5 grams X 4 = 2 calories

Carbohydrate: 15 grams X 4 = 60 calories

Fat: 9.8 grams X 9 = 88 calories

Sodium: 213 milligrams

1% of calories are from protein

40% of calories are from carbohydrate

59% of calories are from fat

The fat content of this product is very high. It is not a good choice as a carbohydrate.

Chicken Bologna, 1 ounce

Calories: 83

Protein: 4 grams X 4 = 16 calories

Carbohydrate: 1 gram X 4 = 4 calories

Fat: 7 grams X 9 = 63 calories

Sodium: 290 milligrams

19% of calories are from protein

5% of calories are from carbohydrate

76% of calories are from fat

The fat content of bologna is very high. Also, it contains corn syrup solids, dextrose, sodium phosphate, sodium erythorbate and sodium nitrite. It is not a good food choice.

Avoiding Unsafe Additives, Preservatives and Artificial Ingredients.

It is best to read labels and avoid certain additives. Although monosodium glutamate occurs naturally in some foods, it is wise not to ask for more: do not buy products with MSG. Certain artificial colors are not safe, especially blue dyes numbers 1 and 2, citrus red number 2, green number 3, red numbers 3 and 40, and yellow number 5. Also avoid sodium nitrate and sodium nitrite. Likewise, do not buy products with brominated vegetable oil (BVO), added caffeine and quinine.

Jane Brody advises us to question the safety of the following: artificial coloring yellow number 6, artificial flavorings, butylated hydroxyanisole (BHA), butylated hydroxytoluene (BHT), carrageenan, heptyl paraben, mono-and diglycerides, phosphoric acid and phosphates, propyl gallate, sodium bisulfate and sulfur dioxide (Brody, p. 487).

My conclusion is that it is wise to avoid these substances.

Some individuals will point out that there are dangerous chemicals which naturally occur in some foods. For example, aflatoxin is often found in peanuts and corn. However, just because there might be naturally found chemicals which are of questionable safety does not mean that we have to go out of our way to *add* ingredients which are artificial and potentially hazardous to our health or the health of our family.

Artificial Sweeteners

In this book, you will find I have not used artificial sweeteners. My flavors come from using good quality vegetables and fruits. People often say, "no salt, no sugar, no fat, no taste." I beg to differ with this idea, since full flavored ingredients will sharpen your taste buds to appreciate what food really tastes like. If you buy apples with excellent flavor, your recipes using apples will taste wonderful. If you buy or grow tomatoes with full flavor, your tomato sauces will be outstanding. It is unfortunate that sometimes tomatoes look red and tasty, but have no flavor. Sometimes this is caused by picking tomatoes too early and keeping them in cold storage.

ORGANIC PRODUCE

In addition to cutting down on fats, cholesterol, protein and sodium at the same time that we consume more complex carbohydrates, vegetables and fruits, it is advisable to avoid as much pesticide as we can. I choose to either grow vegetables and fruits organically or purchase food (when available) which is certified organically grown. In California, labels will read "organically grown and processed in accordance with Sec. 26,569.11 Calif. Health and Safety Code."

DIABETES EXCHANGES

Six diabetes exchanges have been developed by the American Diabetes Association and the American Dietetic Association to help people with diabetes plan their meals (1). The basic idea is that it is best to distribute carbohydrates, proteins and fats throughout the day, rather than overeating at one time and under-eating at another. Meal plans based on the exchanges prevent high concentrations of calories bombarding the body at one time. By this method, the person with diabetes has a tool to help control blood sugar levels. Exercise and insulin or oral medication are also essential tools helping regulate blood sugar.

The categories are as follows: starch/bread (about 80 calories per exchange), meat/fish (about 55 to 100 calories per exchange, depending on the fat content), vegetable (about 25 calories per exchange), fruit (about 60 calories per exchange), milk (about 80 to 150 calories per exchange, depending on the fat content), and fat (about 45 calories per exchange). In addition, there is a list of free foods containing items with very low calories.

The starch/bread exchange includes approximately 1/2 cup cereal and 1 slice of bread. The meat exchange includes lean, medium fat, and high fat meats, as well as fish, cheese, and eggs. One exchange of meat, fish or poultry is about 1 ounce.

You will notice that some recipes in this book contain no meat but are still classified under the meat/fish exchange. The vegetable exchange includes about 1/2 cup cooked vegetables or 1 cup raw vegetables. The fruit exchange contains about 1/2 cup of fruit. There is an expanded list in Chapter 8, DESSERTS. The milk exchange includes 1 cup of milk. The fat exchange includes about 1 teaspoon of oil, mayonnaise or other high fat content foods. The free list contains coffee, tea, and clear broth, certain low calorie vegetables, sugar substitutes, and herbs and spices.

You will find that some foods on the exchange lists, such as those containing saturated fat, are not recommended by the guidelines discussed above. In addition, some foods are on the free exchange list but still have to be considered individually as to their real "free" character. For example, clear broth often contains protein which must be added to the grams of protein eaten each day by people adopting a low protein diet.

Thus, just because food items are listed in the diabetes exchanges does not mean that we should consume them. Consider the diabetes exchanges as a framework for planning your meals and snacks so you can avoid eating too much or too little at any one time during the day. Many people without diabetes find this framework valuable in planning a well rounded diet geared to avoid periods of over consumption alternating with starvation to "make up for binges."

The diabetes exchanges listed after each recipe in this book are based on the exchange which most closely fits the nutritional composition of the ingredients in the recipe.

Today, many people with diabetes do not follow the diabetes exchange plan in strict fashion. There may be variations in eating according to the amount of exercise and activity, as well as according to the particular needs of each individual. These variations are best discussed with your physician and dietitian.

You will find that many of the serving sizes used in the nutritional analysis are small, since they are based on the idea of the exchange system. Many meal plans are designed by a dietitian to contain 2 starches, 2 fruits or 2 meat/fish. You certainly have the choice of eating a larger portion than one exchange, if that would approximate your meal plan and calorie intake per day for maintaining good weight.

For all people, whether having diabetes or not, the concept of exchanges provides an excellent tool to help decide on the size of food portions.

GREASING PANS

To cut down on the amount of fat, especially saturated fat in our diet, I suggest using a small amount of canola oil (less than 1/2 teaspoon usually works) to prevent food from sticking to baking or muffin pans. You might also use a non-stick pan with a small amount of canola oil.

KOSHER RECIPES

I have followed kosher guidelines in the creation of the recipes in this book.

There is no use of shellfish or pork products and no mixing of milk with meat.

Now you are on your own. Remember that the recipe is a guide. The type and shape of the pans used, the kind of ingredients used, the humidity and temperature of the kitchen, and the shelf in the oven used are all factors in the way your product will turn out.

Learn how to adjust the seasonings suggested in the recipe to your own taste. I wish you luck, and I hope the philosophy in this book will lead you to improve your health and enrich the quality of your life.

Judith Caditz, Ph.D.
March, 1992

REFERENCES

1. American Diabetes Association and the American Dietetic Association, *Exchange Lists for Meal Planning.* Available in large print.

2. National Academy Press. *Diet and Health: Implications for Reducing Chronic Disease Risk.* Washington, D.C., 1989.

3. "Nutritional Recommendations and Principles for Individuals with Diabetes Mellitus." *Diabetes Care.* 14 (Supplement 2) 20-27, 1991.

These recommendations also appear in every month's issue of *Diabetes Forecast.*

4. American Heart Association, "Dietary Guidelines for Healthy American Adults," *Circulation.* Vol. 77, No. 3, March 1988.

5. American Cancer Society, "Taking Control: 10 Steps to a Healthier Life and Reduced Cancer Risk," 1985.

6. U.S. Department of Health and Human Services, *The Surgeon General's Report on Nutrition and Health.* Publication No. 88-50211, 1988.

7. Jane Brody, *Jane Brody's Nutrition Book.* New York: Bantam Books, 1982.

CHAPTER 1

SOUPS

BEAN SOUP

1 cup pinto beans

4 cups water

4 cups TOMATO PURÉE (p. 69)

1 chopped onion

1 chopped carrot

1 cup chopped celery, with tops

2 teaspoons SALT FREE SEASONING (p. 51), or 1/2 teaspoon each of oregano and basil, 1/4 teaspoon each of ginger, thyme, garlic powder and ginger, and 1/8 teaspoon pepper

3/4 cup unfiltered apple juice

1/3 cup red wine or apple cider vinegar

- Soak beans overnight in pot of water covering beans with an extra 4 inches of water.
- Discard this water and add 4 cups water to the pot.
- Add puréed tomatoes, onion, carrot, celery, and seasoning.
- Bring to a boil, lower temperature and simmer for 2 hours, stirring occasionally.
- Add apple juice and vinegar and stir.
- If you wish thicker soup, take half of the mixture and mash the beans. Return to the pot, stir, and serve.

- Place extra soup in labeled and dated freezer containers.
- Soup may be thawed and reheated in a microwave.

Yield: about 8 cups soup. One serving: 1/2 cup.

Per serving:

calories	64
protein	3.1 grams
fat	0.3 grams
carbohydrate	13.0 grams
fiber	2.5 grams
cholesterol	0 milligrams
sodium	14 milligrams

Diabetes exchanges:

1 starch

<table>
<tr>
<td>

FOR VARIETY:

Use kidney, black, navy, great north-ern or small white beans, or a mixture.

</td>
<td>

LOW VISION TIP #1:

Cook soups over medium heat to avoid a hard boil which may cause spatters.

</td>
</tr>
</table>

BEET SOUP (BORSCHT)

4 cups beets, quartered with greens
3 cups water
2 tablespoons lemon juice
1/3 cup unfiltered apple juice

- Cut fibrous ends off beets and cut into quarters.
- Steam until a fork pierces them and slip off outer skins if you wish.
- Cut off the tough portions of the greens and steam them separately (they will take less time).
- Chop beets and greens and place in a large pot with water.
- Simmer for about 10 minutes.
- Add lemon and apple juices.

Yield: 3-1/2 cups soup. One serving: 1 cup.

Per serving:

calories 36
protein . . . . 1.2 grams
fat . . . . 0.5 grams
carbohydrate . . . . 8.0 grams
fiber . . . . 1.0 grams
cholesterol . . . . 0 milligrams
sodium . . . . 67 milligrams

Diabetes exchanges:

1 vegetable

SERVING SUGGESTION:

Serve warm or cold. Serve with boiled or steamed potato and non-fat plain yogurt.

BLACK BEAN-BARLEY SOUP

1 cup black beans

1/3 cup barley

5 cups water

1/2 cup unfiltered apple juice

1/3 cup chopped onions

1/3 cup sliced mushrooms

1 teaspoon dry mustard

1/2 teaspoon cloves

1/2 teaspoon thyme

1/8 teaspoon ground black pepper

1/4 teaspoon salt (optional, add 36 milligrams sodium per serving)

1/4 cup red wine vinegar or apple cider vinegar

- Soak beans overnight in water to cover the beans by 4 inches.

- Rinse beans and place them in pot with 5 cups water.

- Bring to a boil, lower heat and simmer 1 hour. If you wish, you may remove half of the beans, mash them, and return the mashed beans to the pot.

- Add apple juice, onions, mushrooms, mustard, cloves, thyme, pepper and salt (if used) and simmer for an additional hour.

- **Add vinegar.**

Yield: 8 cups of thick soup. One serving: 1/2 cup.

Per serving:

calories 63
protein . . . . 3.1 grams
fat . . . . 0.3 grams
carbohydrate . . . . 12.5 grams
fiber . . . . 2.4 grams
cholesterol . . . . 0 milligrams
sodium . . . . 2 milligrams

Diabetes exchanges:

1 starch

LOW VISION TIP #2:

Cover soup pot with a tilted lid to help prevent spatters.

CABBAGE SOUP

3 cups water

4 cups cabbage, shredded

1/3 cup sliced carrots

1/3 cup chopped onions

1-1/2 teaspoons SALT FREE SEASONING (p. 51), or 1/4 teaspoon each of basil, oregano, cloves, thyme, celery seed and dill and 1/8 teaspoon pepper

1 cup unfiltered apple juice

2 tablespoons lemon juice

- Place water, cabbage, carrots, onions, and seasoning in a large pot.
- Bring to a boil, reduce heat and simmer until water level drops down to less than 1 inch (about 20 minutes).
- Stir in apple and lemon juices and simmer for an additional 25 minutes.

Yield: about 4 cups of soup. One serving: 1 cup.

Per serving:

calories 60
protein . . . . 1.3 grams
fat . . . . 0.3 grams
carbohydrate . . . . 14.4 grams
fiber . . . . 2.5 grams
cholesterol . . . . 0 milligrams
sodium . . . . 20 milligrams

Diabetes exchanges:

2 vegetable

SERVING SUGGESTION:

You may add boiled potato, brown or basmati rice or whole wheat pasta to the soup.

CHICKEN SOUP

1 fryer chicken, 2-1/2 pounds, cut into parts with skin and fat removed

2 onions

2 carrots

2 celery stalks with leaves

1/4 teaspoon salt (optional, add 72 milligrams sodium per serving)

- Place ingredients into a pot with 3 quarts of water and boil.
- Reduce heat to moderate and cook for 2 hours, or until chicken is cooked thoroughly.
- Let cool and strain soup through colander lined with cheesecloth.
- Reserve the chicken, onions, carrots, and celery to add to chicken soup, chicken croquettes, chicken loaf or pasta salad.
- Place soup in refrigerator and cool for several hours or overnight.
- Remove all fat which has formed on top.

Yield: about 8 cups of soup. One serving: 1 cup of clear broth.

Per serving:

calories	22
protein	4.9 grams
fat	0.0 grams
carbohydrate	1.9 grams
fiber	0.0 grams
cholesterol	0 milligrams
sodium	5 milligrams

Diabetes exchanges:

free*

*If you are on a low protein diet, please note the amount of protein in 1 cup.

SERVING SUGGESTION: *Soup may be served as clear broth, with matzo balls, noodles, or rice and with pieces of chicken, onions, carrots, and celery from the cooking.*	**CHICKEN BROTH CUBES:** *Place clear chicken broth in ice cube tray in the freezer. Use for stove top or wok cooking.*

MATZO BALLS

1/2 cup matzo meal*

1 egg

2 egg whites

1 tablespoon defatted chicken soup

1/2 teaspoon canola oil

1/4 teaspoon salt (optional, add 96 milligrams sodium per serving)

- Mix matzo meal with salt (if used).
- Mix egg with egg whites and beat lightly.
- Add chicken soup and oil to egg mixture.
- Sprinkle matzo meal into egg mixture, stirring constantly with a fork to prevent lumps.
- Refrigerate for 1/2 hour.
- Boil 3 quarts of water.
- Dampen hands with cold water and shape mixture into balls about 1 or 2 inches in diameter.
- Drop balls into water, reduce heat, cover and bring to a gentle boil again.
- Simmer for 45 minutes.
- Remove matzo balls from water with a slotted spoon and add to heated chicken soup.

Yield: 12 matzo balls. One serving: 2 matzo balls.

*If you prefer whole grains, try pulverizing whole wheat matzo in the food processor. Now you have whole wheat matzo meal. The calculations below are based on whole wheat matzo meal.

Per serving:

calories	52
protein	3.2 grams
fat	1.6 grams
carbohydrate	6.3 grams
fiber	1.3 grams
cholesterol	37 milligrams
sodium	32 milligrams

Diabetes exchanges:

1 starch

SERVING SUGGESTION:

Excellent for holiday meals. Matzo balls may also be added to other soups.

LENTIL SOUP

1 cup lentils

3 cups water

2 cups TOMATO PURÉE (p. 69)

1/2 cup chopped onions

1/2 cup chopped carrots

1/4 cup chopped celery, including leaves

1-1/2 teaspoons of SALT FREE SEASONING (p. 51), or 1/2 teaspoon each of thyme, oregano and basil and 1/8 teaspoon pepper

2 tablespoons lemon juice

- Place lentils in pot of boiling water.
- Reduce heat to a slow boil, and cook about 45 minutes until lentils are soft but not mushy.
- Add tomatoes, onions, carrots, celery and seasoning and cook an additional 30 minutes.
- Stir in lemon juice.

Yield: About 6 cups soup. One portion: 1/2 cup.

Per serving:

calories 69
protein . . . . 5.0 grams
fat . . . . 0.3 grams
carbohydrate . . . . 12.4 grams
fiber . . . . 2.6 grams
cholesterol . . . . 0 milligrams
sodium . . . . 9 milligrams

Diabetes exchanges:

1 starch

LOW VISION TIP #3:

If you use a microwave to thaw and warm frozen soups, you might mark the temperature setting with Hi Dot. This raised dot makes it possible for you to feel the correct setting.

Inquire at the low vision center in your area about where to buy these raised dot markers.

SPLIT PEA SOUP

1 cup split peas

5 cups water

1/3 cup chopped onions

1 teaspoon SALT FREE SEASONING (p. 51), or
1/4 each of thyme, oregano, basil and cloves and
1/8 teaspoon pepper

2 tablespoons unseasoned rice vinegar

- Add split peas to 5 cups of boiling water.
- Reduce heat and stir.
- Add onion, celery and seasoning and simmer for 45 minutes or until peas are tender.
- Add vinegar and simmer another 20 minutes.
- Let soup cool a while and purée in a blender or food processor.

Yield: makes 4 cups of soup.
One serving: 1/2 cup.

Per serving:

calories 88
protein . . . . 6.2 grams
fat . . . . 0.3 grams
carbohydrate . . . . 15.8 grams
fiber . . . . 1.5 grams
cholesterol . . . . 0 milligrams
sodium . . . . 4 milligrams

Diabetes exchanges:

1 starch
1/2 lean meat/fish

SERVING SUGGESTION:

*Include BUCKWHEAT GROATS (p. 121) or
BROWN RICE (p. 152) with your meal.*

SPLIT PEA-TOMATO SOUP

1 cup split peas

3 cups water

2 bay leaves

2 cups TOMATO PURÉE (p. 69)

1/2 cup chopped onions

1/2 cup chopped carrots

1/2 cup chopped celery with leaves

1 teaspoon SALT FREE SEASONING (p. 51), or
1/4 teaspoon each of thyme, basil, oregano and
ginger and 1/8 teaspoon pepper

2 tablespoons red wine vinegar or apple cider
vinegar

- Bring water to a boil, add split peas and lower heat.

- Add bay leaves and simmer for 30 minutes, stirring occasionally.

- Add tomatoes, onions, carrots, celery and seasoning and continue cooking for another 30 minutes, or until peas are tender. If a thinner soup is desired, add a little more water.

- Remove bay leaves and stir in vinegar.

- If you wish, you may take half the soup and purée it in a food processor or blender and return to the pot.

Yield: 6 cups thick soup. One serving: 1/2 cup.

Per serving:

calories 69
protein . . . . 4.5 grams
fat . . . . 0.3 grams
carbohydrate . . . . 12.9 grams
fiber . . . . 1.7 grams
cholesterol . . . . 0 milligrams
sodium . . . . 12 milligrams

Diabetes exchanges:

1 starch

SERVING SUGGESTION:

Try whole wheat pasta with the soup.

VEGETABLE SOUP WITH BARLEY

6 cups water

2 cups quartered tomatoes

1 cup chopped carrots

1 cup chopped leek (white portion only)

1/2 cup chopped onions

1/4 cup chopped celery with tops

1/2 cup barley

2 teaspoons SALT FREE SEASONING (p. 51), or 1/2 teaspoon each of thyme and basil, 1/4 teaspoon each of oregano, ginger, dry mustard and cloves and 1/8 teaspoon pepper

1/4 cup unfiltered apple juice

1/8 cup unseasoned rice vinegar

- Place water in large pot and add tomatoes, carrots, leeks, onion, celery, barley and seasoning.
- Bring to a boil, reduce heat and simmer for 1 hour and 10 minutes, or until barley is cooked.
- Add apple juice and vinegar and stir.

Yield: 10 cups of soup. One serving: 1/2 cup.

Per serving:

calories	32
protein	0.9 grams
fat	0.2 grams
carbohydrate	7.1 grams
fiber	1.4 grams
cholesterol	0 milligrams
sodium	7 milligrams

Diabetes exchanges:

1/2 starch

SERVING SUGGESTION:

You may serve this hearty soup with
BEANS (p. 114).

CHAPTER 2

SALADS

BEAN-RICE SALAD

1 cup cooked PINTO BEANS (p. 114)
1 cup cooked BROWN RICE (p. 152)
1/2 cup diced celery with tops
1/2 cup diced carrots
1/2 cup diced tomatoes
1/2 cup chopped onions
1/4 cup chopped parsley
4 tablespoons TOMATO BASED DRESSING (p. 53)

- Mix beans, rice and vegetables together and add dressing.

Yield: about 4 cups. One serving: 1/2 cup.

Per serving:

calories	70
protein	2.8 grams
fat	0.4 grams
carbohydrate	14.1 grams
fiber	2.1 grams
cholesterol	0 milligrams
sodium	14 milligrams

Diabetes exchanges:

1 starch

FOR VARIETY:

Use kidney, black, navy, great north- ern or white beans, or a mixture.

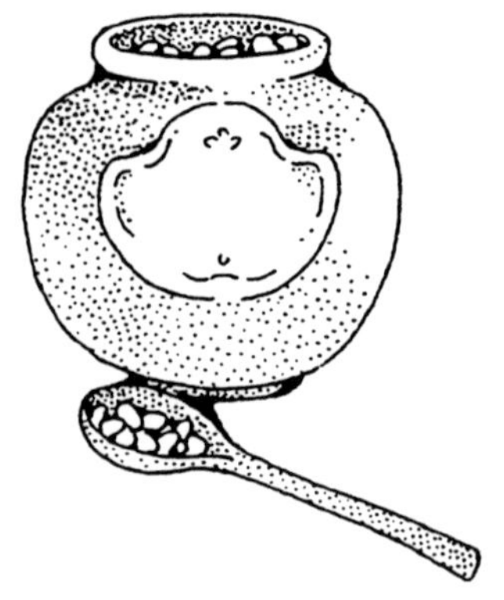

CARROT SALAD

2 cups grated carrots

1/3 cup raisins

2 tablespoons lemon juice

* Mix ingredients together.

Yield: about 2 cups. One serving: 1/4 cup.

Per serving:

calories 31
protein . . . . 0.5 grams
fat . . . . 0.1 grams
carbohydrate . . . . 7.9 grams
fiber . . . . 1.2 grams
cholesterol . . . . 0 milligrams
sodium . . . . 10 milligrams

Diabetes exchanges:

1 vegetable

FOR VARIETY:

Add 1 grated apple, 1/2 cup non-fat plain yogurt, or 1 small can unsweetened crushed pineapple (drain juice if the salad has too much liquid).

CHICKEN-PASTA SALAD

6 ounces cooked chicken breast with skin and visible fat removed

1 cup cooked pasta spirals, well drained (whole wheat, no cholesterol and no sodium)

1 tomato, cut into wedges

4 leaves of romaine or red leaf lettuce, broken into pieces

3 radishes, sliced

2 green onions, cut into small pieces

1/2 cup bean sprouts

1/2 cup alfalfa sprouts

1 cucumber sliced with skin

several leaves of radicchio

1/2 cup celery with tops, diced

1 carrot, sliced thinly

1/2 cup sliced water chestnuts

6 parsley sprigs

2 tablespoons lemon juice

1/4 cup NO OIL VINAIGRETTE DRESSING (p. 55)

- Cut chicken into small pieces.
- Mix all ingredients together and add dressing.
- For full flavor, refrigerate several hours before serving.

Yield: about 8 cups. One serving: 2 cups.

Per serving:

calories	174
protein	17.4 grams
fat	2.2 grams
carbohydrate	22.9 grams
fiber	2.5 grams
cholesterol	36 milligrams
sodium	67 milligrams

Diabetes exchanges:

1 starch
1-1/2 lean meat/fish
1-1/2 vegetable

FOR VARIETY:

Substitute turkey, cooked or canned salmon, or tofu for chicken.

Use LOW OIL VINAIGRETTE DRESSING (p. 54) or TOMATO BASED DRESSING (p. 53).

COLE SLAW

1 cup grated green cabbage

1 cup grated red cabbage

1 cup grated apple

1/2 cup grated carrots

1/4 cup chopped scallions, with greens

1/4 cup chopped parsley

DRESSING

3 tablespoons unfiltered apple juice

2 tablespoons lemon juice

2 tablespoons unseasoned rice vinegar

1/4 teaspoon dill

- Toss cabbage, carrots, apple, scallions and parsley.
- Combine dressing ingredients and stir into cabbage mixture.

Yield: about 3-1/2 cups. One serving: 1/2 cup.

Per serving:

calories	25
protein	0.5 grams
fat	0.1 grams
carbohydrate	6.4 grams
fiber	1.4 grams
cholesterol	0 milligrams
sodium	7 milligrams

Diabetes exchanges:

1 vegetable

FOR VARIETY:

Use YOGURT DRESSING (p. 56)

LOW VISION TIP #5:

Organize all items in your kitchen so you know where to find them. Return to the same place to store.

LENTIL-GREEN BEAN SALAD

1 cup cooked LENTILS (p. 137)
1/2 cup green onions with greens, chopped
several leaves romaine or red leaf lettuce
1 cup lightly steamed string beans
2 tomatoes, cut into wedges
1 carrot, sliced
few sprigs of watercress
2 tablespoons NO OIL VINAIGRETTE DRESSING
(p. 55)

- Combine lentils and onions.
- Place on leaves of lettuce.
- Make a circle around the lentils with tomatoes, string beans, carrots and watercress.
- Sprinkle with dressing.

Yield: about 2-1/4 cups. One serving: 3/4 cup.

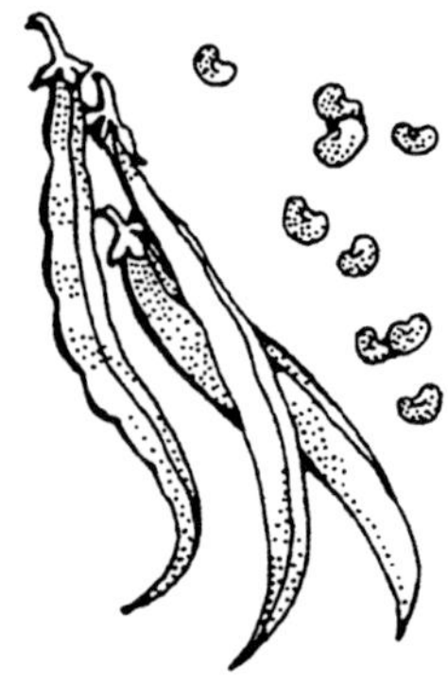

Per serving:

calories 175
protein . . . . 12.6 grams
fat . . . . 0.8 grams
carbohydrate . . . . 32.4 grams
fiber . . . . 7.9 grams
cholesterol . . . . 0 milligrams
sodium . . . . 29 milligrams

Diabetes exchanges:

2 starch
1 lean meat/fish
1 vegetable

FOR VARIETY:

*Use LOW OIL VINAIGRETTE DRESSING (p. 54)
or TOMATO BASED DRESSING (p. 53).*

LIMA BEAN SALAD

1 package of frozen baby lima beans (10 ounces), steamed

2 tablespoons NO OIL VINAIGRETTE DRESSING (p. 55)

1/8 cup slivered almonds (optional, add 7.5 calories and 0.7 grams of fat per serving)

* Mix dressing with lima beans and sprinkle with almonds.

Yield: 2 cups. One serving: 1/3 cup.

Per serving:

calories	51
protein	3.2 grams
fat	0.2 grams
carbohydrate	9.5 grams
fiber	2.5 grams
cholesterol	0 milligrams
sodium	14 milligrams

Diabetes exchanges:

1/2 starch

SERVING SUGGESTION:	**FOR VARIETY:**
Serve cold or warm as a side dish.	*Use LOW OIL VINAIGRETTE DRESSING (p. 54).*

NOODLE SALAD

1 cup cooked, rinsed, and well drained whole wheat noodles, no cholesterol and no sodium

1 cup steamed string beans

1 cup steamed zucchini

1 cup steamed carrots

4 tablespoons NO OIL VINAIGRETTE DRESSING (p. 55)

- Mix ingredients together.
- Add dressing.

Yield: 4 cups. One serving: 1 cup.

Per serving:

calories	75
protein	3.1 grams
fat	0.4 grams
carbohydrate	16.8 grams
fiber	1.9 grams
cholesterol	0 milligrams
sodium	16 milligrams

Diabetes exchanges:

1 starch

FOR VARIETY:

Use LOW OIL VINAIGRETTE DRESSING (p. 54), TOMATO BASED DRESSING (p. 53), YOGURT DRESSING (p. 56) or YOGURT HOOP CHEESE DRESSING (p. 57).

SERVING SUGGESTION:

Serve cold as a main course, or serve warm as a side dish.

LOW VISION TIP #6:

Work in a kitchen with good lighting.

PASTA SALAD

5 ounces (dry) spiral whole wheat pasta, no cholesterol or sodium

1 cup steamed broccoli pieces

1 cup steamed sliced carrots

1 cup steamed sliced red, green, and yellow sweet peppers

2 tablespoons pine nuts

1/2 cup NO OIL VINAIGRETTE DRESSING (p. 55)

- Cook pasta according to directions on package.
- Steam vegetables until slightly underdone, not mushy. It is best to steam each type of vegetable separately, since they take a different amount of cooking time.
- Gently toss pasta with vegetables, pine nuts and dressing.

Yield: about 3-1/2 cups. One serving: 1 cup.

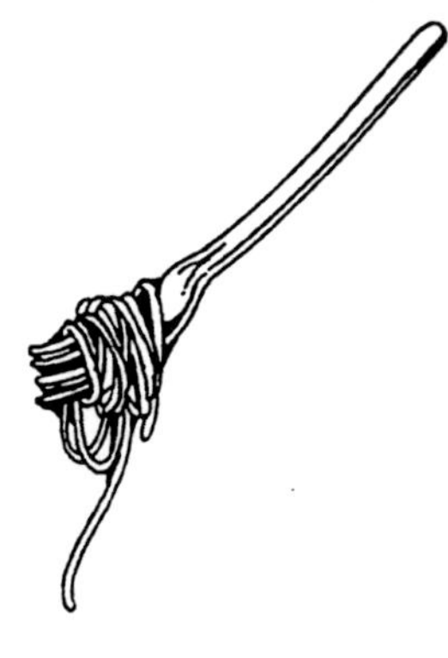

Per serving:

calories 104
protein . . . . 4.3 grams
fat . . . . 1.9 grams
carbohydrate . . . . 20.1 grams
fiber . . . . 3.6 grams
cholesterol . . . . 0 milligrams
sodium . . . . 12 milligrams

Diabetes exchanges:

1 starch
1 vegetable

<table>
<tr>
<td>

SERVING SUGGESTION:

Serve cold as a salad, or warm as a main course dish.

</td>
<td>

FOR VARIETY:

Use LOW OIL VINAIGRETTE DRESSING (p. 54) or TOMATO BASED DRESSING (p. 53).

</td>
</tr>
</table>

BLACK EYED PEAS AND BUCKWHEAT GROATS SALAD

1/2 cup cooked BLACK EYED PEAS (p. 116)
1/2 cup cooked BUCKWHEAT GROATS (p. 121)
1/2 cup celery, diced
1/2 medium onion, chopped
few sprigs of parsley, chopped
4 tablespoons NO OIL VINAIGRETTE DRESSING
(p. 55)*

- Combine ingredients.

Yield: 2 cups. One serving: 1/2 cup.

Per serving:

calories	48
protein	2.2 grams
fat	0.3 grams
carbohydrate	10.2 grams
fiber	4.0 grams
cholesterol	0 milligrams
sodium	16 milligrams

Diabetes exchanges:

1 starch

*FOR VARIETY: Use LOW OIL VINAIGRETTE
DRESSING (p. 54).

POTATO SALAD

4 new potatoes, cut up and steamed until fork pierces

1 medium onion, chopped

6 sprigs of parsley, chopped

2 tablespoons YOGURT DRESSING (p. 56)

- Cut potatoes into small pieces and mix with onion and parsley.
- Add YOGURT DRESSING

Yield: about 3 cups. One serving: 3/4 cup.

Per serving:

calories	114
protein	2.6 grams
fat	0.2 grams
carbohydrate	26.3 grams
fiber	2.3 grams
cholesterol	0 milligrams
sodium	10 milligrams

Diabetes exchanges:

2 starch

FOR VARIETY:

Use NO OIL VINAIGRETTE DRESSING (p. 55) or LOW OIL VINAIGRETTE DRESSING (p. 54).

BROWN RICE-WILD RICE SALAD

2 cups cooked BROWN RICE (p. 152)

1/4 cup cooked WILD RICE (p. 152)

2 tablespoons NO OIL VINAIGRETTE DRESSING (p. 55)

* Mix ingredients together and serve cold.

Yield: 2-1/2 cups. One serving: 1/2 cup.

Per serving:

calories	112
protein	2.5 grams
fat	0.8 grams
carbohydrate	23.6 grams
fiber	1.0 grams

(+ additional fiber for wild rice, information not available)

cholesterol	0 milligrams
sodium	3 milligrams

Diabetes exchanges:

1-1/2 starch

FOR VARIETY:

Use LOW OIL VINAIGRETTE DRESSING (p. 54).

SALMON SALAD

1 can salmon, 7-1/2 ounces (no salt added)

1/2 cup non-fat plain yogurt

1/2 cup diced celery

1 tablespoon lemon juice

1 tablespoon unseasoned rice vinegar

1 tablespoon lemon juice

Several sprigs parsley cut into small pieces

Several leaves romaine or red leaf lettuce

- Mix ingredients together and serve on a bed of lettuce.
- You may substitute fresh poached, baked or broiled salmon.

Yield: about 1 cup. One serving: 1/3 cup.

Per serving:

calories	126
protein	16.4 grams
fat	4.4 grams
carbohydrate	4.8 grams
fiber	0.3 grams
cholesterol	1 milligram
sodium	99 milligrams

Diabetes exchanges:

2 lean meat/fish; 1 vegetable

TOFU SALAD

4 ounces tofu

1 teaspoon low sodium soy sauce or tamari

1 teaspoon canola oil

- Cut tofu into pieces.
- Sprinkle canola oil on skillet and place tofu in pan.
- Set heat on moderate, sprinkle soy sauce on top, and brown on one side.
- Turn and brown on second side.

MIXED SALAD

1/2 head romaine or red leaf lettuce, torn into pieces

1 tomato, cut into wedges

1/2 cup celery, cut up

few sprigs of parsley

1/2 cup coarsely grated carrots

1/4 cup snow peas

1/2 cup string beans, steamed lightly

1/2 cup asparagus, steamed lightly

4 tablespoons NO OIL VINAIGRETTE DRESSING (p. 55)

- Combine salad ingredients.
- Place tofu on top of mixed salad and dresssing.

Yield: about 4 cups of salad. One serving: 1 cup of salad.

Per serving:

calories	70
protein	4.8 grams
fat	2.9 grams
carbohydrate	8.2 grams
fiber	3.1 grams
cholesterol	0 milligrams
sodium	68 milligrams

Diabetes exchanges:

1/2 starch
1/2 lean meat/fish

FOR VARIETY:

Use TOMATO BASED DRESSING (p. 53).

TUNA-EGG WHITE SALAD

1 can unsalted tuna packed in water, 6 ounces

2 hard boiled and chopped egg whites

2 tablespoons lemon juice

2 tablespoons non-fat plain yogurt

1/2 cup chopped green onions

1/4 cup alfalfa sprouts

* Combine ingredients and serve on a bed of lettuce.

Yield: about 1-1/4 cup. One serving: 1/4 cup.

Per serving:

calories	59
protein	12.0 grams
fat	0.2 grams
carbohydrate	1.9 grams
fiber	0.3 grams
cholesterol	0 milligrams
sodium	44 milligrams

Diabetes exchanges:

1-1/2 lean meat/fish

SERVING SUGGESTION:

May be served on whole grain toast.

CHOPPED RAW VEGETABLE SALAD

1/2 cup diced carrots

1/2 cup broccoli, cut into small pieces

1/4 cup scallions with greens, chopped

1 diced tomato

1/2 cup bean sprouts

1/2 cup diced celery

1/2 cup tender, young string beans

1/2 cup zucchini, crooked neck squash, or summer squash, cut into pieces

1/2 cup chopped cauliflower

1/4 cup chopped sweet red pepper

4 tablespoons NO OIL VINAIGRETTE DRESSING (p. 55)

several leaves of romaine lettuce

1 turnip, sliced

Few sprigs of watercress

- Combine ingredients.
- Add dressing and serve on a bed of lettuce. Trim with turnip and watercress.

Yield: about 4 cups. One serving: 1 cup.

Per serving:

calories 50
protein . . . . 2.6 grams
fat . . . . 0.4 grams
carbohydrate . . . . 11.3 grams
fiber . . . . 3.3 grams
cholesterol . . . . 0 milligrams
sodium . . . . 51 milligrams

Diabetes exchanges:

2 vegetable

FOR VARIETY:

Lightly steam vegetables or mix raw and steamed vegetables.

Use LOW OIL VINAIGRETTE DRESSING (p. 54) or TOMATO BASED DRESSING (p. 53).

CHAPTER 3

DRESSINGS AND SAUCES

DRESSINGS

SALT FREE SEASONING

2 teaspoons basil
2 teaspoons celery seed
2 teaspoons cloves
2 teaspoons coriander
2 teaspoons cumin
2 teaspoons garlic powder
1 teaspoon ginger
1 teaspoon marjoram
1 teaspoon dry mustard
2 teaspoons onion powder
2 teaspoons oregano
2 teaspoons dried parsley
1/2 teaspoon pepper
1 teaspoon rosemary
1/2 teaspoon sage
2 teaspoons tarragon
2 teaspoons thyme

- Combine ingredients.
- Place in jar with tight lid and store in cool, dry area.

free

If you prefer to buy a salt free seasoning, there are several available in the market.

LOW VISION TIP #7:

Place herbs and spices in alphabetical order and keep them in the same order. If you have difficulty reading the labels, you can find them by counting the number of containers from the left or right.

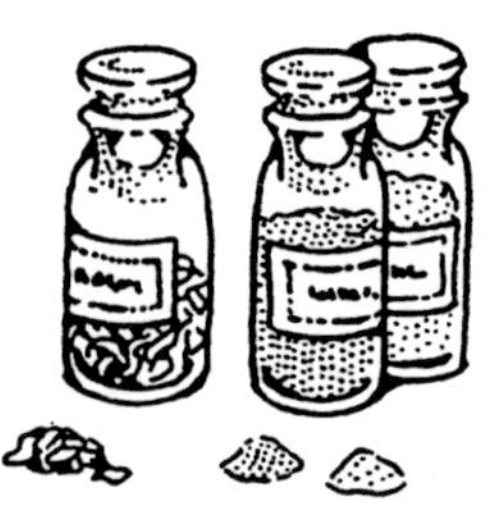

TOMATO BASED DRESSING

1/2 cup TOMATO PURÉE (p. 69)

1/4 cup red wine vinegar

1 tablespoons olive oil (optional, add 7 calories and 0.9 grams fat per serving)

1 teaspoon basil

1 teaspoon oregano

1 teaspoon garlic powder

1/4 cup unfiltered apple juice

- Mix ingredients together and place in bottle.

Yield: about 4 cups. One serving: 4 tablespoons (1/4 cup).

Per serving:

calories	4
protein	0.0 grams
fat	0.0 grams
carbohydrate	1.2 grams
fiber	0.0 grams
cholesterol	0 milligrams
sodium	0 milligrams

Diabetes exchanges:

1/2 vegetable

VINAIGRETTE DRESSING (LOW OIL)

1 cup unseasoned rice vinegar or red wine vinegar
2 tablespoons olive oil
1 teaspoon oregano
1 teaspoon basil
1 teaspoon mustard (no salt)
1 tablespoon horseradish (uncreamed)
2 tablespoons unfiltered apple juice

* Mix ingredients together and place in refrigerator several hours before serving.

Yield: about 1-1/4 cups. One serving: 1/8 cup (2 tablespoons).

Per serving:

calories	33
protein	0.1 grams
fat	3.1 grams
carbohydrate	2.1 grams
fiber	0.1 grams
cholesterol	0 milligrams
sodium	2 milligrams

Diabetes exchanges:

1/2 fat

VINAIGRETTE DRESSING
(NO OIL)

The same as **VINAIGRETTE DRESSING (LOW OIL)** on previous page, but do not add oil.

Per serving:

calories 3
fat 0.0
protein . . . . 0.0 grams
carbohydrate . . . . 1.1 grams
fiber . . . . 0.0 grams
cholesterol . . . . 0 milligrams
sodium . . . . 1 milligram

Diabetes exchanges:

free

YOGURT DRESSING

1/2 cup non-fat plain yogurt

2 tablespoons lemon juice

1/4 teaspoon oregano

1/4 teaspoon basil

1/4 teaspoon dill

1 teaspoon dry mustard

1 tablespoon unseasoned rice vinegar

1 tablespoon unfiltered apple juice

1 teaspoon uncreamed horseradish

- Combine ingredients.

Yield: about 1 cup dressing. One serving: 1/8 cup (2 tablespoons).

Per serving:

calories	12
protein	1.0 grams
fat	0.2 grams
carbohydrate	2.0 grams
fiber	0.0 grams
cholesterol	0 milligrams
sodium	12 milligrams

Diabetes exchanges:

free

YOGURT-HOOP CHEESE DRESSING AND DIP

4 ounces unsalted hoop cheese

3 ounces plain non-fat yogurt

1 finely chopped scallion, with greens

2 tablespoons lemon juice

2 tablespoons unfiltered apple juice

6 sprigs parsley, finely chopped

1/2 teaspoon dill weed

- Combine all ingredients.
- Place in refrigerator several hours before serving.
- Use within two days.

Yield: 1 cup dressing. One portion: 1/4 cup (4 tablespoons).

Per serving:

calories	40
protein	5.9 grams
fat	0.3 grams
carbohydrate	4.1 grams
fiber	0.2 grams
cholesterol	2 milligrams
sodium	21 milligrams

1/2 skim milk

LOW VISION TIP #8:

A set of measuring spoons kept tied together will be helpful. Some people like the type with long handles to reach to the bottom of containers.

SERVING SUGGESTION:

Use as a dip for hors d'oeuvres.

SAUCES

APPLESAUCE

6 apples
juice of 2 lemons
1/2 cup unfiltered apple juice

- Peel and quarter apples and sprinkle with lemon juice.
- Place apples and apple juice in pot and cook over medium heat for about 15 minutes, or until fork penetrates.
- Mash apples until a chunky consistency, or purée in food processor for a short time for a finer texture.

Yield: about 2 cups. One serving: 1/2 cup

Per serving:

calories	130
protein	0.4 grams
fat	0.6 grams
carbohydrate	34.0 grams
fiber	5.1 grams
cholesterol	0 milligrams
sodium	1 milligram

Diabetes exchanges:

2 fruit

PEAR SAUCE:

Substitute cut up pears for apples.

SERVING SUGGESTION:

Excellent combined with main dish vegetables, fish, chicken, turkey or pasta.

CRANBERRY-APPLE SAUCE

1-1/4 cup sweet apples, cut into small pieces
1 cup unfiltered apple juice
1 cup cranberries
1 tablespoon lemon juice
1 package unflavored gelatin

- Place cut up apples in large pot with 3/4 cup apple juice and cook over medium heat for 5 minutes, until apples are just tender.
- Add cranberries and lemon juice and cook another 10 minutes, or until cranberries pop open.
- Stir in lemon juice.
- Mash mixture with a fork or blend in a food processor for less than a minute, so that the cranberries and apples are still somewhat lumpy.
- Set into a medium sized bowl.
- In a separate small pot place 1/4 cup apple juice and warm over low heat for a few minutes.
- Stir in gelatin and keep stirring until it is melted.
- Mix melted gelatin with cranberries and apples and place in a container in the refrigerator until jelled.

Yield: about 1-2/3 cups sauce.
One portion: 1/3 cup.

Per serving:

calories	54
protein	1.4 grams
fat	0.2 grams
carbohydrate	12.7 grams
fiber	1.2 grams
cholesterol	0 milligrams
sodium	3 milligrams

Diabetes exchanges:

1/2 fruit

SERVING SUGGESTION:

Very good with poultry or fish.

PLUM SAUCE

2 cups plums, quartered and pressed into measuring cup

I-1/2 packages unflavored gelatin

juice of 1 lemon

1 can prune juice, 5-1/2 fluid ounces

1/2 cup unfiltered apple juice

- Place plums in medium saucepan and cook over medium heat for 10 minutes, or until soft, but not overcooked.

- If plum skins taste bitter, remove them.

- Mash plums slightly with fork. If you wish, you may purée plums in food processor.

- In a small saucepan, warm apple juice over low heat and sprinkle in gelatin, stirring with a fork so that no lumps will form. Stir until gelatin is melted.

- Add gelatin mixture to apple, lemon and prune juices.

- Stir thoroughly into plums.

- Place in refrigerator for several hours until sauce is jelled.

Yield: about 3-1/2 cups. One serving: 1/2 cup.

Per serving:

calories 58
protein . . . . 1.8 grams
fat . . . . 0.3 grams
carbohydrate . . . . 13.0 grams
fiber . . . . 1.3 grams
cholesterol . . . . 0 milligrams
sodium . . . . 3 milligrams

Diabetes exchanges:

1 fruit

FOR VARIETY:

To make APRICOT SAUCE substitute apricots for plums. To make PEACH SAUCE substitute peaches for plums.

SALSA

1 cup TOMATO PURÉE (p. 69)

1 cup quartered plum tomatoes

1 chopped onion

1/2 cup carrot pieces

1/2 cup chopped parsley

1-1/2 teaspoons SALT FREE SEASONING (p. 51)

1-2 teaspoons chili powder

1/4 cup unfiltered apple juice

- Combine ingredients.
- Place in medium saucepan, bring to a boil, reduce heat and simmer for about 45 minutes.
- Stir occasionally.

Yield: about 3 cups. One serving: 4 tablespoons (1/4 cup).

Per serving:

calories 20
protein . . . . 0.8 grams
fat . . . . 0.0 grams
carbohydrate . . . . 4.4 grams
fiber . . . . 0.8 grams
cholesterol . . . . 0 milligrams
sodium . . . . 8 milligrams

Diabetes exchanges:

1 vegetable

SERVING SUGGESTION:

Use with pasta, beans and vegetables.

TOMATO SAUCE

2 cups plum tomatoes, puréed

1 chopped onion

2 tablespoons lemon juice

1/2 cup chopped parsley

1-1/2 teaspoons SALT FREE SEASONING (p. 51)

1/4 cup unfiltered apple juice

- Combine ingredients.
- Place in medium saucepan, bring to a boil, reduce heat and simmer for about 45 minutes.
- Stir occasionally.

Yield: about 2 cups. One serving: 4 tablespoons (1/4 cup).

Per serving:

calories 25
protein . . . . 0.8 grams
fat . . . . 0.2 grams
carbohydrate . . . . 5.7 grams
fiber . . . . 1.0 grams
cholesterol . . . . 0 milligrams
sodium . . . . 7 milligrams

Diabetes exchanges:

1 vegetable

TOMATO PURÉE:

Cut fresh tomatoes into quarters and simmer until soft. Mash or place in food processor and purée. If you use canned tomatoes, buy those <u>without salt and sugar.</u>

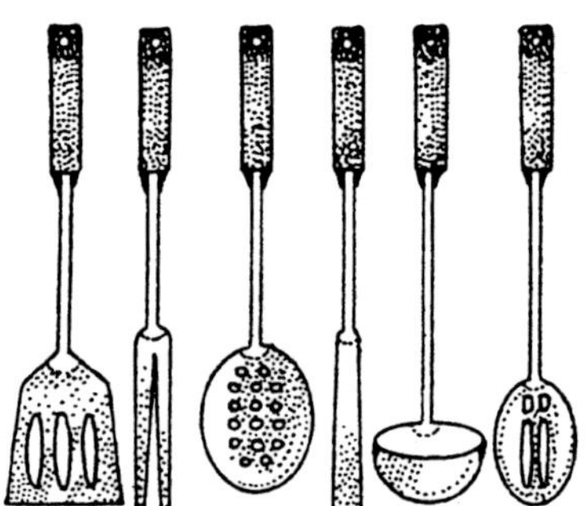

CHAPTER 4

FISH, POULTRY
AND BEEF

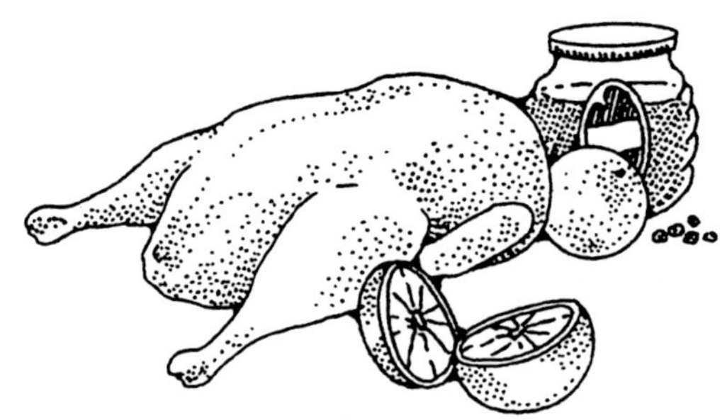

STUFFED CABBAGE ROLLS

8 leaves of green cabbage

8 ounces ground turkey, skin and fat removed before grinding

3/4 cup cooked brown rice

1/2 cup chopped onions

1/4 cup chopped shallots

1/3 cup chopped parsley

2 teaspoons SALT FREE SEASONING (p. 51), or 1/2 teaspoon each of oregano and basil, 1/4 teaspoon each of ginger, thyme, nutmeg and mustard, and 1/8 teaspoon pepper

6 frozen cubes of defatted chicken broth

2 tablespoons unseasoned rice vinegar

2 tablespoons unfiltered apple juice

- Cut out the end of the cabbage.
- Carefully separate 8 large outer leaves.
- Place them in a pot with 2 inches of boiling water and simmer until the leaves will bend without breaking.
- Mix ground turkey with onions, shallots, parsley and seasoning.
- Set two chicken broth cubes in a skillet over medium heat.

- Stir in the turkey mixture and add more chicken broth cubes as needed.
- When turkey is cooked, stir in brown rice.
- Add apple juice and vinegar and stir thoroughly.
- Spoon about two tablespoons of the mixture into each cabbage leaf.
- Fold each leaf into a roll and place in a lightly greased baking pan.
- Cover with aluminum foil and bake in an oven preheated to 325 for 30 minutes.

Yield: 8 cabbage rolls. One serving: 1 roll.

Per serving:

calories	83
protein	6.1 grams
fat	2.4 grams
carbohydrate	9.1 grams
fiber	1.1 grams
cholesterol	21 milligrams
sodium	33 milligrams

Diabetes exchanges:

1/2 starch
1 lean meat/fish

LOW VISION TIP #9:

Some people find it easier to use a microwave to loosen cabbage leaves than to boil water. Cut out the bottom core of the cabbage by cutting in a circle. Set the cabbage head in a microwave on a custard cup with a few tablespoons of water. Separate the leaves as they become pliable.

FOR VARIETY:

Cover with SALSA (p. 66) or TOMATO PUREE (p. 69).

CHICKEN AND COLLARDS

- **Prepare VEGETARIAN COLLARDS (p. 128). Add 4 ounces cut up chicken (broiled, baked, poached, or soup chicken) with skin and all visible fat removed.**

Yield: about 2 cups. One serving: 1/2 cup.

Per serving:

calories	96
protein	9.1 grams
fat	4.5 grams
carbohydrate	5.0 grams
fiber	0.7 grams
cholesterol	25 milligrams
sodium	32 milligrams

Diabetes exchanges:

1 lean meat/fish
1 vegetable

FOR VARIETY:

Use chard, kale or spinach instead of collards.

CHICKEN BREAST WITH MUSTARD SAUCE

2 chicken breasts, 3-1/2 ounces each, bones, skin and fat removed

1 teaspoon lemon juice

mustard sauce

MUSTARD SAUCE FOR CHICKEN

1/4 cup unfiltered apple juice

1-1/2 teaspoons dry mustard

1 tablespoon unseasoned rice vinegar

1 tablespoon whole wheat flour

1 teaspoon uncreamed horseradish

1/2 teaspoon garlic powder

- Place chicken in baking pan and sprinkle with lemon juice.
- Blend all ingredients in mustard sauce and pour over chicken.
- Set the pan in the refrigerator for 1 hour.
- Place pan in oven preheated to 350 degrees and bake for 45 minutes.

- Cover pan with aluminum foil and continue baking for an additional 30 minutes, or until chicken is done.

Yield: 2 chicken breasts.
One serving: 1 chicken breast.

Per serving:

calories	109
protein	14.3 grams
fat	2.1 grams
carbohydrate	7.9 grams
fiber	0.6 grams
cholesterol	36 milligrams
sodium	35 milligrams

Diabetes exchanges:

1-1/2 lean meat/fish

ENVIRONMENTAL TIP:

Aluminum foil may be washed and reused.
If not usable, recycle.

CHICKEN BREAST WITH TOMATO-CUCUMBER SAUCE

2 chicken breasts, 4 ounces each, skin and fat removed

juice of one lemon

1 teaspoon SALT FREE SEASONING (p. 51), or 1/4 teaspoon each thyme, basil, garlic powder and dry mustard and 1/8 teaspoon pepper

TOMATO-CUCUMBER SAUCE

1/2 cup SALSA (p. 66)
1/4 cup sliced pickling cucumbers

- **Place chicken breasts in casserole and sprinkle with lemon juice and seasoning.**
- **Mix salsa and cucumbers together and pour over chicken.**
- **Place covered casserole in oven preheated to 350 degrees and bake for 1 hour and 15 minutes, or until chicken is done (a piece will come off easily with a fork).**

Yield: 2 chicken breasts with sauce.
One serving: 1 chicken breast with sauce.

Per serving:

calories 85
protein . . . . 13.5 grams
fat . . . . 3.2 grams
carbohydrate . . . . 3.7 grams
fiber . . . . 0.6 grams
cholesterol . . . . 36 milligrams
sodium . . . . 66 milligrams

Diabetes exchanges:

1 lean meat/fish
1 vegetable

SERVING SUGGESTION:

Excellent with beans, rice or pasta.

CHICKEN CROQUETTES

3 cups chicken from chicken soup, bones and skin removed

1-1/2 cup onions, carrots, and celery from chicken soup

1/2 cup oat bran

2 tablespoons defatted chicken broth (if needed)

- Blend chicken, onions, carrot and celery in a food processor (do not overprocess).
- Add oat bran.
- Add chicken broth if needed.
- Shape mixture into balls and place them in a baking dish lightly greased with canola oil.
- Bake in oven preheated to 325 degrees for about 30 minutes.
- Turn croquettes and complete baking in about 10 minutes, or until browned.

Yield: about 12 croquettes 3-1/2 inches in diameter. One serving: 1 croquette.

SERVING SUGGESTION:

Serve with APPLESAUCE (p. 60).

Per serving:

calories 83
protein . . . . 11.1 grams
fat . . . . 2.9 grams
carbohydrate . . . . 4.0 grams
fiber . . . . 1.0 gram
cholesterol . . . . 32 milligrams
sodium . . . . 37 milligrams

Diabetes exchanges:

1 lean meat/fish
1 vegetable

FOR VARIETY:

CHICKEN LOAF. *Place mixture into non-stick loaf pan lightly greased with canola oil.*

Bake in oven preheated to 325 degrees for 40 minutes.

Yield: about 12 slices. One serving: 1 slice.

CHICKEN STIR FRY

2 chicken breasts, 4 ounces each, boned, skinned and frozen

2 teaspoons canola oil

6 frozen cubes of defatted chicken broth

1/4 cup of each vegetable, thinly sliced: carrots, potatoes, zucchini, mushrooms, onions, celery, cabbage, sweet pepper, and leek (total of 2-1/4 cups)

1/4 cup China pea pods

1/4 cup string beans, cut into 1 inch pieces

1/2 cup broccoli, broken into small pieces

1/2 teaspoon grated ginger

1/4 cup shallots, sliced thinly

1/2 cup bean sprouts

1/4 cup water chestnuts, sliced thinly

1 teaspoon SALT FREE SEASONING (p. 51), or 1/4 teaspoon each of oregano, basil, thyme, mustard, and 1/8 teaspoon pepper

---

- Partially thaw chicken breasts and slice thinly.
- Place canola oil and two cubes of chicken broth in wok or large skillet and stir fry chicken.
- Remove chicken and place in a bowl.
- Stir fry vegetables with seasonings and ginger. Add bean sprouts and water chestnuts last.

- Add more chicken cubes as needed.
- Return the chicken to the wok or skillet and stir everything together for a few seconds. Serve immediately.

Yield 6 cups. One serving: 1 cup.

Per serving:

calories	102
protein	10.7 grams
fat	2.8 grams
carbohydrate	8.7 grams
fiber	1.6 grams
cholesterol	24 milligrams
sodium	36 milligrams

Diabetes exchanges:

1 lean meat/fish
2 vegetable

<table>
<tr><td>SERVING SUGGESTION:

Serve with steamed rice, buckwheat groats or noodles.</td><td>LOW VISION TIP #10:

Cook stir fry over medium or low medium heat to avoid spattering.</td></tr>
</table>

BEEF STIR FRY

- Use the recipe for CHICKEN STIR FRY (p. 83) but substitute 8 ounces lean rib steak for chicken.
- Freeze the meat, partially thaw, and cut into thin slices.
- Proceed to cook the same as CHICKEN STIR FRY.

Yield: about 6 cups. One serving: 1 cup.

Per serving:

calories	119
protein	9.7 grams
fat	5.0 grams
carbohydrate	8.8 grams
fiber	1.6 grams
cholesterol	23 milligrams
sodium	35 milligrams

Diabetes exchanges:

1 medium fat meat/fish
2 vegetable

CHICKEN TOSTADA

4 corn tortillas, no salt added, 6 inches in diameter

4 ounces cooked chicken, skin and fat removed, cut up

1/2 cup cooked beans

1/2 cup cooked tomatoes, chunky

1/3 cup sliced onions

1/4 cup chopped sweet pepper

1 or 2 teaspoons chili powder

1/2 teaspoon cumin

1/4 teaspoon dry mustard

2 medium fresh tomatoes

several lettuce leaves

- Warm tortillas in oven or microwave.
- Place chicken, beans, tomatoes, onions, pepper, chili powder, cumin and mustard in a skillet.
- Simmer for 15 minutes until all flavors are blended.
- Place a heaping tablespoon of chicken-bean mixture on tortilla.
- Garnish with fresh tomatoes and lettuce.

Yield: 4 tostadas. One serving: 1 tostada.

Per serving:

calories	180
protein	13.5 grams
fat	3.9 grams
carbohydrate	24.4 grams
fiber	4.0 grams
cholesterol	25 milligrams
sodium	42 milligrams

Diabetes exchanges:

1 starch
1 lean meat/fish
2 vegetable

SERVING SUGGESTION:

Tasty with BROWN or BASMATI RICE (p. 152).

GEFILTE FISH (FISH BALLS)

3 pounds white fish, separate bones and skin

1 pound pike, carp, or trout, separate bones and skin

3 white onions

I carrot

3 celery stalks

I egg and 3 egg whites

2 tablespoons matzo meal or oat bran

I/2 teaspoon salt (optional, add 48 milligrams sodium per serving)

I/4 teaspoon ground pepper or to taste

I/4 cup ice water

- **FISH STOCK**: Add fish bones and skin, 2 onions, carrot, and stalk of celery to 3 quarts of water, and simmer while preparing the fish.*

- **GRIND FISH**. If you use a food processor, first cut the fish into small pieces (2 inches by 2 inches). This is easily done if the fish is frozen first and then partially thawed.

- Add 1 chopped onion.

- Mix egg with egg whites and add to mixture.

- Mix salt (if used) and pepper with matzo meal or oat bran and add to mixture.

- Add ice water.

- Dip hands into cold water and shape fish mixture into balls, about 2 by 3 inches. Be careful to handle fish gently so it does not become too compact.
- Place fish into gently boiling stock, cover and cook over moderate heat (with water slightly bubbling) for 45 minutes. Tip the lid of the pot as the fish is cooking.
- Remove fish from stock with slotted spoon and place in pan and refrigerate.

Yield: about 12 fish balls each weighing about 3 ounces. One serving: 1 fish ball.

* You may strain the fish stock, removing bones and skin, and return the liquid to the pot. Reheat stock so that it is boiling gently and add the fish. Cook for 45 minutes.

Per serving:

calories	64
protein	11.1 grams
fat	0.8 grams
carbohydrate	2.4 grams
fiber	0.2 grams
cholesterol	40 milligrams
sodium	45 milligrams

Diabetes exchanges:

1-1/2 lean meat/fish

SERVING SUGGESTIONS:

Serve with horseradish. Place on plate with lettuce, a slice of carrot from fish stock and a tomato wedge.

Traditionally served at holiday meals. Also delicious as a main course for lunch or dinner.

BAKED HALIBUT

1 piece of halibut, 6 ounces

MUSTARD SAUCE FOR FISH

3 teaspoons prepared mustard (without salt)

1 teaspoon SALT FREE SEASONING (p. 51), or 1/4 each of thyme, basil, tarragon and garlic powder and 1/8 teaspoon pepper

1 tablespoon whole wheat flour

2 tablespoons unfiltered apple juice

1 teaspoon uncreamed horseradish

1/8 teaspoon paprika (sprinkle on top of sauce)

- Blend all sauce ingredients together.
- Place halibut in lightly greased loaf pan (about 8 by 5 by 2-1/2 inches) and pour the sauce over the fish.
- Bake in oven preheated to 350 degrees for 20 minutes.
- Cover with aluminum foil and cook an additional 10 minutes, or until fish flakes off with a fork.

Yield: 2 portions of fish and sauce.
One serving: 1/2 the amount of cooked fish.

Per serving:

calories	113
protein	18.2 grams
fat	2.2 grams
carbohydrate	4.0 grams
fiber	0.5 grams
cholesterol	40 milligrams
sodium	48 milligrams

Diabetes exchanges:

2 lean meat/fish
1 vegetable

FOR VARIETY:

*Use TOMATO CUCUMBER-SAUCE
(from CHICKEN WITH TOMATO-CUCUMBER
SAUCE p. 79)*

ORANGE ROUGHY

1/2 cup fresh mushrooms, sliced

1/4 cup shallots, chopped

1 piece of orange roughy, 6 ounces

1/2 teaspoon paprika

2 tablespoons lemon juice

1/4 cup sliced water chestnuts

- Cook mushrooms and shallots for 10 minutes over medium heat in covered skillet with 2 tablespoons water.
- Place orange roughy over mushrooms and shallots and sprinkle with paprika and lemon juice.
- Add water chestnuts, cover and cook about 15 minutes, or until fish flakes off with a fork.

Yield: 4 ounces of fish. One serving: 2 ounces of fish plus vegetables.

Per serving:

calories 148
protein . . . . 13.7 grams
fat . . . . 6.1 grams
carbohydrate . . . . 9.5 grams
fiber . . . . 0.6 grams
cholesterol . . . . 17 milligrams
sodium . . . . 59 milligrams

Diabetes exchanges:

1/2 starch
2 lean meat/fish

FOR VARIETY:

Use MUSTARD SAUCE (from BAKED HALIBUT p. 91) or TOMATO CUCUMBER SAUCE (from CHICKEN WITH CUCUMBER SAUCE p. 79).

LOW VISION TIP #11:

Be careful to close kitchen cabinet doors immediately after getting out what you need to avoid bumps to the head.

POACHED SALMON

1 salmon steak, 5 ounces
1/2 cup TOMATO PURÉE (p. 69)
1/2 cup chopped onions
1/4 cup chopped celery with tops
1/4 cup chopped shallots
1 tablespoon lemon juice
1 tablespoon unfiltered apple juice
1/2 teaspoon SALT FREE SEASONING (p. 51)

- Place salmon in non-stick skillet.
- Combine all other ingredients and pour over salmon.
- Simmer on medium heat for 30 minutes, or until salmon flakes off with a fork.

Yield: 1 salmon steak and sauce.
One serving: 1/2 steak and sauce.

Per serving:

calories 171
protein . . . . 17.2 grams
fat . . . . 6.3 grams
carbohydrate . . . . 12.0 grams
fiber . . . . 1.2 grams
cholesterol . . . . 36 milligrams
sodium . . . . 55 milligrams

Diabetes exchanges:

1/2 starch
2-1/2 lean meat/fish

FOR VARIETY:

Add 1/2 cup sliced mushrooms to skillet.

SNAPPER POACHED IN TOMATOES

1 snapper fillet, 9 ounces
1 cup TOMATO PURÉE (p. 69)
1/4 cup chopped onions
1 cup thinly sliced zucchini
1 teaspoon SALT FREE SEASONING (p. 51), or 1/4 teaspoon each of oregano, basil, tarragon and thyme and 1/8 teaspoon pepper

- Place tomato purée and onions in large non-stick skillet and simmer for 5 minutes.
- Add snapper and sprinkle with seasoning.
- Add zucchini, simmer for 15 minutes and turn snapper over.
- Simmer for an additional 10 minutes.
- The snapper is done if the thickest part flakes off with a fork.

Yield: 4 portions. One serving: 1/4 of fish and sauce.

Per serving:

calories 83
protein . . . . 14.0 grams
fat . . . . 1.1 grams
carbohydrate . . . . 4.2 grams
fiber . . . . 1.0 grams
cholesterol . . . . 24 milligrams
sodium . . . . 46 milligrams

Diabetes exchanges:

2 lean meat/fish
1 vegetable

FOR VARIETY:

Add 1/4 cup sliced shallots and 1/4 cup sliced mushrooms.

FILLET OF SOLE

1 piece fillet of sole, 6 ounces

2 tablespoons lemon juice

2 tablespoons oat bran

2 tablespoons corn meal

1 teaspoon SALT FREE SEASONING (p. 51), or 1/4 teaspoon each of garlic powder, onion powder, basil and dry mustard and 1/8 teaspoon pepper

* Sprinkle lemon juice on sole.

* On a separate plate, mix together oat bran, corn meal and seasoning.

* Dip both sides of fish in mixture and place in lightly greased loaf pan (about 8 by 5 by 2-1/2 inches).

* Set in oven preheated to 350 degrees and bake for about 30 minutes, or until fish flakes off with a fork.

Yield: 4 ounces of fish. One serving: 2 ounces of fish.

Per serving:

calories	131
protein	18.0 grams
fat	1.7 grams
carbohydrate	12.6 grams
fiber	1.5 grams
cholesterol	41 milligrams
sodium	70 milligrams

Diabetes exchanges:

1 starch
2 lean meat/fish

FOR VARIETY:

Try with TOMATO CUCUMBER SAUCE (from CHICKEN WITH CUCUMBER SAUCE p. 79) or MUSTARD SAUCE (from BAKED HALIBUT p. 91). Flounder is a good substitute for sole.

HAWAIIAN TUNA STEAK

l fresh tuna steak, 4 ounces

1 tablespoon unsweetened crushed pineapple

1 teaspoon unsweetened pineapple juice

1 tablespoon lemon juice

1 teaspoon low sodium soy sauce

1 teaspoon SALT FREE SEASONING (p. 51), or
1/4 teaspoon each of dry mustard, tarragon, basil
and thyme and 1/8 teaspoon pepper

* Lightly grease a pie pan or another small baking dish and place tuna in pan.

* Combine pineapple, pineapple juice, lemon juice, soy sauce and seasoning and sprinkle mixture on fish.

* Set the baking dish into the oven preheated to 350 degrees.

* Bake for 15 minutes and turn steak.

* Cover with aluminum foil and bake for an additional 10 minutes, or until steak flakes off with a fork.

Yield: 2 portions. One serving: 1/2 baked fish.

Per serving:

calories 92
protein . . . . 13.6 grams
fat . . . . 2.9 grams
carbohydrate . . . . 2.3 grams
fiber . . . . 0.2 grams
cholesterol . . . . 22 milligrams
sodium . . . . 103 milligrams

Diabetes exchanges:

2 lean meat/fish

SERVING SUGGESTION:

Good with baked potato, non-fat plain yogurt and chopped scallions.

GROUND TURKEY COCKTAIL NUGGETS

1/2 lb. ground turkey, skin and fat removed before grinding.

1/4 cup chopped onions

1/4 cup chopped sweet pepper

1/4 cup chopped celery

1/4 cup grated potatoes

1/4 cup grated carrots

1 teaspoon uncreamed horseradish

1 teaspoon SALT FREE SEASONING (p. 51), or 1/4 teaspoon each of ginger, thyme, nutmeg and oregano and 1/8 teaspoon pepper

1/2 cup oat bran

- Combine onions, pepper, celery, potatoes, carrots and horseradish with ground turkey.

- Mix seasoning with oat bran and add to ground turkey mixture.

- Shape into balls (about 30) and place under broiler for 10 minutes on one side and 3 minutes on the other.

- Add to the sauce.

SAUCE

1 cup TOMATO PURÉE (p. 69)

1/2 cup unsweetened crushed pineapple, with juice

1/4 cup apple cider vinegar

1/4 cup unfiltered apple juice

1 tablespoon lemon juice

- Combine all ingredients.
- Cook in saucepan over medium heat for 10 minutes.
- Add ground turkey rounds.
- Simmer for 10 minutes and serve (warm or cold).

Yield: 30 cocktail nuggets.
One serving: 2 nuggets.

Per serving:

calories	35
protein	4.0 grams
fat	0.8 grams
carbohydrate	5.2 grams
fiber	0.9 grams
cholesterol	5 milligrams
sodium	15 milligrams

Diabetes exchanges:

1/2 lean meat/fish
1 vegetable

GROUND BEEF COCKTAIL NUGGETS

- Follow the recipe for GROUND TURKEY COCK-TAIL NUGGETS (p. 103).
- Substitute 1/2 pound lean ground chuck for ground turkey.
- Use the same sauce.

Yield: 30 nuggets. One serving: 2 nuggets.

Per serving:

calories	54
protein	5.4 grams
fat	1.8 grams
carbohydrate	5.2 grams
fiber	0.9 grams
cholesterol	10 milligrams
sodium	14 milligrams

Diabetes exchanges:

1/2 lean meat/fish

1 vegetable

SERVING SUGGESTION:

Use as hors d'oeuvres.

GROUND TURKEY LOAF

1/2 pound ground turkey, all skin and fat removed before grinding

1/2 cup grated potatoes

1/4 cup TOMATO PURÉE (p. 69)

1/4 cup chopped onions

1/4 cup chopped sweet pepper (green, red, orange, or yellow)

2 tablespoons chopped parsley

1/2 teaspoon thyme

1/2 teaspoon cloves

1/4 teaspoon ginger

1/8 teaspoon pepper, or to taste

- Combine potato, tomatoes, onions, sweet pepper, parsley and seasoning.
- Mix with ground turkey.
- Place in lightly greased loaf pan (about 8 by 5 by 2-1/2 inches), cover and bake for 25 minutes in oven preheated to 350 degrees.
- Cover with aluminum foil until ready to serve.

Yield: 1 loaf about 7-1/2 by 4-1/2 by 1-1/2 inches. One serving: 1/4 loaf.

Per serving:

calories 81
protein . . . . 12.7 grams
fat . . . . 1.9 grams
carbohydrate . . . . 6.4 grams
fiber . . . . 0.9 grams
cholesterol . . . . 19 milligrams
sodium . . . . 41 milligrams

Diabetes exchanges:

1 lean meat/fish
2 vegetable

SERVING SUGGESTION:

CRANBERRY-APPLE SAUCE (p. 62) goes well with this dish.

GROUND BEEF LOAF

- Use the same recipe as GROUND TURKEY LOAF (p. 106).

- Substitute 1/2 pound of lean ground chuck for turkey.

Yield: 1 loaf. One serving: 1/4 of loaf.

Per serving:

calories	150
protein	17.9 grams
fat	5.6 grams
carbohydrate	6.4 grams
fiber	0.9 grams
cholesterol	49 milligrams
sodium	39 milligrams

Diabetes exchanges:

1 medium fat meat/fish
2 vegetable

CHAPTER 5

VEGETABLES, GRAINS, PASTA AND BEANS

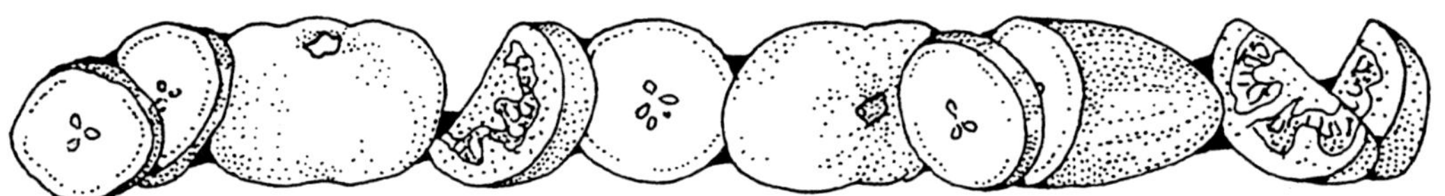

ASPARAGUS WITH SHALLOTS

2 cups asparagus, tough ends removed

1/2 cup shallots, thinly sliced

2 tablespoons lemon juice

1 tablespoon **NO OIL VINAIGRETTE DRESSING** (p. 55)

- Steam asparagus (either whole or cut up) until just tender.
- Sautèe shallots in skillet with 2 tablespoons of water.
- Combine asparagus and shallots, sprinkle with lemon juice and seasoning and serve.

Yield: about 2 cups. One serving: 1 cup.

Per serving:

calories	38
protein	4.9 grams
fat	0.8 grams
carbohydrate	15.2 grams
fiber	0.9 grams
cholesterol	0 milligrams
sodium	7 milligrams

Diabetes exchanges:

2 vegetable

AZUKI BEANS AND PASTA

1/2 cup azuki beans

1/2 cup whole wheat pasta (no sodium or cholesterol), broken into 1 inch pieces

6 cups water

1 cup TOMATO PURÉE (p. 69)

1/4 cup chopped onions

1/4 cup unseasoned rice vinegar

2 egg whites, slightly beaten

3 tablespoons unfiltered apple juice

2 teaspoons olive oil

1 teaspoon SALT FREE SEASONING (p. 51), or 1/4 teaspoon each of oregano, cumin, garlic powder and dry mustard and 1/8 teaspoon pepper

* Soak beans for 4 hours, or overnight covered by 4 inches of water.

* Pour off liquid and place beans in large pot with 6 cups of water.

* Bring to a boil again and simmer until beans are tender, about 25 minutes.

* Drain the beans. They should measure about 1-1/4 cups.

* Cook pasta according to directions on package (should measure 1-1/2 cups when drained).

- Combine beans and pasta and add tomatoes, onions, vinegar, apple juice, olive oil and seasonings.
- Mix in egg whites and bake in lightly greased loaf pan (about 8 by 5 by 2-1/2 inches) for 50 minutes until done.

Yield: about 4 cups. One serving: 1/2 cup.

Per serving:

calories	89
protein	4.6 grams
fat	1.4 grams
carbohydrate	15.5 grams
fiber	1.2 grams
cholesterol	0 milligrams
sodium	16 milligrams

Diabetes exchanges:

1 starch

BEANS (PINTO)

1 cup beans

3 cups water

1/8 teaspoon salt (optional, add 96 milligrams sodium per serving)

- Place beans in a pot and add water to cover by 4 inches. Soak overnight.
- Drain water and add fresh water to cover by 4 inches.
- Bring to a boil and simmer for 1-1/2 to 2 hours, or until tender.

Yield: about 3 cups. One serving: 1/3 cup.

Per serving:

calories	109
protein	6.7 grams*
fat	0.4 grams
carbohydrate	20.4 grams
fiber	3.9 grams
cholesterol	0 milligrams
sodium	3 milligrams

Diabetes exchanges:

1 starch

*for those on low protein diets, please note the amount of protein.

FOR VARIETY:

You may sustitute any other dried bean for pinto beans, but notice the low vision tip below.

LOW VISION TIP #12:

Use larger beans. Set measured amount in a bowl and transfer them a few at a time to another bowl. This technique will help you eliminate any pebbles sometimes found in the package.

BLACK EYED PEAS

1/2 cup black eyed peas

1-1/2 cup water

1/8 teaspoon salt (optional, add 72 milligrams sodium per serving)

- Bring water with peas to a boil, reduce heat, and simmer covered for about 20 minutes or until peas are tender.

Yield: 2 cups. One serving: 1/2 cup.

Per serving:

calories	70
protein	4.9 grams
fat	0.3 grams
carbohydrate	12.5 grams
fiber	1.6 grams
cholesterol	0 milligrams
sodium	3 milligrams

Diabetes exchanges:

1 starch

BROCCOLI RICE BAKE

2 cups broccoli flowerettes, measured after steaming and chopping

1 cup cooked BROWN RICE (p. 152)

1/2 cup grated apple

1/2 cup chopped onions

4 ounces hoop cheese

1/4 cup chopped parsley

2 teaspoons SALT FREE SEASONING (p. 51), or 1/2 teaspoon each of oregano, basil, thyme and tarragon and 1/8 teaspoon pepper

1 tablespoon lemon juice

4 egg whites, beaten moderately

- Steam broccoli and chop.
- Add rice, apple, onions, hoop cheese, parsley, seasoning and lemon juice.
- Add egg whites.
- Place mixture in lightly greased 9 inch pie pan.
- Bake in oven preheated to 350 for 10 minutes.
- Reduce heat to 325 degrees and bake an additional 20 minutes.

Yield: 4 portions. One serving: 1/4 of pie.

Per serving:

calories 134
protein . . . . 11.0 grams
fat . . . . 1.0 gram
carbohydrate . . . . 21.5 grams
fiber . . . . 2.8 grams
cholesterol . . . . 2 milligrams
sodium . . . . 71 milligrams

Diabetes exchanges:

1 starch
1 lean meat/fish
1 vegetable

SERVING SUGGESTION:

Good as a main course with
MIXED SALAD (p. 43) and
APPLESAUCE (p. 60).

BRUSSELS SPROUTS CASSEROLE

2 cups brussels sprouts

2 cups cauliflower cut into 2 inch sections

1 cup sliced carrots

1/4 cup sliced shallots

1/2 cup pearl onions, steamed lightly to slip off skins

1/2 cup fresh mushrooms, sliced

2 tablespoons lemon juice

1 teaspoon canola oil

2 teaspoons olive oil

1 teaspoon SALT FREE SEASONING (p. 51), or 1/4 teaspoon each of oregano, basil, thyme and ginger and 1/8 teaspoon pepper

1/4 cup sliced water chestnuts

- Steam brussels sprouts for 10 minutes.
- Remove from pot and cut into quarters.
- Spread canola oil on bottom of casserole.
- Put brussels sprouts in casserole and sprinkle with lemon juice.
- Add cauliflower pieces, carrots, shallots, pearl onions and mushrooms.

- Sprinkle with seasoning as you combine ingredients.
- Sprinkle olive oil on vegetables.
- Cover casserole and place in oven preheated to
  325 degrees.
- Bake for 45 minutes, remove cover and stir in
  water chestnuts.
- Complete baking for another 10 minutes, or
  until all vegetables are tender, but not overcooked.

Yield: 5 cups vegetables. One serving: 1 cup.

Per serving:

calories	90
protein	3.2 grams
fat	3.2 grams
carbohydrate	14.8 grams
fiber	4.9 grams
cholesterol	0 milligrams
sodium	31 milligrams

Diabetes exchanges:

3 vegetable
1/2 fat

BUCKWHEAT GROATS (KASHA)

1/2 cup buckwheat groats

1-1/4 cup water

1/8 teaspoon salt (optional, add 72 milligrams sodium per serving)

- Place groats in medium sized pot with water.
- Bring to a boil, reduce heat, and simmer covered for 20 minutes, or until all water is absorbed.

Yield: 2 cups. One serving: 1/2 cup.

Per serving:

calories	71
protein	2.4 grams
fat	0.6 grams
carbohydrate	15.4 grams
fiber	2.0 grams
cholesterol	0 milligrams
sodium	2 milligrams

Diabetes exchanges:

1 starch

LOW VISION TIP #13:

Use a set of measuring cups sized for 1/4, 1/3, 1/2 and 1 cup.

BUCKWHEAT GROATS IN CHICKEN BROTH

1 cup chicken broth, defatted

1/4 cup chopped celery with leaves

1/4 cup chopped onions

1/2 teaspoon SALT FREE SEASONING (p. 51), or 1/4 teaspoon oregano and 1/4 teaspoon dry mustard

1/2 cup buckwheat groats

- Place celery, onions and seasoning in skillet with a few tablespoons of chicken broth.
- Cook over medium heat until just tender. Stir while cooking.
- Place buckwheat groats and chicken broth in a medium pot and bring to a boil.
- Reduce the heat, cover and continue cooking until almost all the water is absorbed (about 15-20 minutes).
- Stir in celery and onions and warm a few more minutes.

Yield: 2 cups. One serving: 1/2 cup.

Per serving:

calories	82
protein	2.7 grams
fat	0.6 grams
carbohydrate	17.0 grams
fiber	3.4 grams
cholesterol	0 milligrams
sodium	10 milligrams

Diabetes exchanges:

1 starch

SERVING SUGGESTION:

This whole grain is good as a side dish and excellent with turkey as a side stuffing.

BUTTERNUT SQUASH BAKE

1 butternut squash, about 5 to 6 inches in diameter

1/2 cup unsweetened crushed pineapple with juice (about 1/2 of small can)

2 tablespoons lemon juice

1/2 teaspoon nutmeg

- Cut squash in half, remove seeds and place in a steaming basket in a pot with 3 inches of water.
- Steam for about 1/2 hour, or until knife will penetrate the shell.
- Let squash cool and scoup out meat of squash.
- Mash with pineapple, lemon juice and nutmeg.
- Place in baking dish and reheat for about 20 minutes.

Yield: about 2 cups squash. One portion: 1/2 cup.

Per serving:

calories 99
protein . . . . 2.1 grams
fat . . . . 0.3 grams
carbohydrate . . . . 25.8 grams
fiber . . . . 2.7 grams
cholesterol . . . . 0 milligrams
sodium . . . . 2 milligrams

Diabetes exchanges:

1 starch
1/2 fruit

SERVING SUGGESTION:

*You may like to roast the seeds and use
as a snack.*

STUFFED CHAPATI

4 whole wheat chapati, no added salt (about 7 inches in diameter each)

1 medium onion, sliced

1/2 sweet pepper, cut up

1/3 cup China peas

1/3 cup bean sprouts

1/3 cup fresh mushrooms, sliced

1/2 cup sliced carrots

4 ounces tofu, cubed

1/2 cup cooked BROWN RICE (p. 152)

1/2 teaspoon SALT FREE SEASONING (p. 51) or equivalent mixture of oregano, basil, dry mustard and cumin and pinch of pepper

1 teaspoon low sodium soy sauce

1 teaspoon canola oil

- Steam vegetables until slightly underdone.
- Mix vegetables with tofu, rice, seasoning, soy sauce, and oil.
- Divide mixture into four portions and place in the center of each chapati.
- Fold stuffed chapati and place with seam down in lightly greased pan.

- Cover with aluminum foil and bake for 15 minutes in oven preheated to 300 degrees.

Yield: 4 stuffed chapati. One serving: 1 chapati.

Per serving:

calories	213
protein	9.7 grams
fat	3.3 grams
carbohydrate	35.4 grams
fiber	5.3 grams
cholesterol	0 milligrams
sodium	90 milligrams

Diabetes exchanges:

2 starch

SERVING SUGGESTION:

Serve as a main dish with citrus fruit.

VEGETARIAN COLLARDS

1 bunch collard greens
1 medium onion, sliced
3 cloves of garlic, minced
1 tablespoon lemon juice
2 teaspoons canola oil

* Wash collards and remove stems.
* Break into 2 to 3 inch pieces and place in a large pot with 1 inch of water.
* Add onion and garlic.
* Bring to a boil and simmer until collards are tender (about 20 minutes).
* Add lemon juice and canola oil and stir.

Yield: about 2 cups. One portion: 1/2 cup.

Per serving:

calories	43
protein	0.9 grams
fat	2.4 grams
carbohydrate	5.0 grams
fiber	0.7 grams
cholesterol	0 milligrams
sodium	8 milligrams

1 vegetable
1/2 fat

FOR VARIETY:

Use chard, kale or spinach instead of collards.

SERVING SUGGESTION:

This "soul food" is excellent as a side dish with fish or poultry.

EGG WHITE VEGETABLE OMELETTE

1/2 teaspoon canola oil

1/4 cup sliced onions

1/4 cup broccoli flowerettes, broken into small pieces

1/4 cup zucchini, sliced

1/4 cup fresh mushrooms, sliced

1 tablespoon chopped shallots

1/2 teaspoon SALT FREE SEASONING (p. 51)

4 egg whites, beaten moderately

- Place canola oil in skillet over moderate heat and add sliced vegetables and seasoning.
- Cover and simmer a short time until vegetables are tender, but not overdone.
- Add egg whites and cover.
- Cook a few minutes until egg whites are done.

Yield: 1-1/2 cups. One serving: 3/4 cup.

Per serving:

calories 65
protein . . . . 8.1 grams
fat . . . . 1.3 grams
carbohydrate . . . . 5.4 grams
fiber . . . . 1.0 grams
cholesterol . . . . 0 milligrams
sodium . . . . 113 milligrams

Diabetes exchanges:

1 lean meat/fish
1 vegetable

SERVING SUGGESTION:

Serve with brown rice, pasta or steamed potatoes.

GREEN BEANS, PEARL ONIONS AND MUSHROOMS

2 cups green beans

1 cup pearl onions

1/2 cups fresh mushrooms, sliced

1 teaspoon SALT FREE SEASONING (p. 51)

- Steam pearl onions until just tender and slip off skins.
- Steam green beans and mushrooms until tender (takes less time than the onions).
- Combine vegetables and toss with seasoning.

Yield: about 3 cups. One serving: 1 cup.

Per serving:

calories	31
protein	1.9 grams
fat	0.1 grams
carbohydrate	7.0 grams
fiber	2.1 grams
cholesterol	0 milligrams
sodium	3 milligrams

Diabetes exchanges:

2 vegetable

KABOCHA SQUASH AND RICE

1 medium kabocha squash, about 6 inches in diameter

1/4 cup cooked wild rice

3/4 cup cooked BROWN or BASMATI RICE (p. 152)

1 teaspoon low sodium soy sauce

1-1/3 teaspoons SALT FREE SEASONING (p. 51), or 1/3 teaspoon each of nutmeg, cloves, cinnamon and ginger and 1/8 teaspoon pepper

6 water chestnuts, sliced

1/4 cup chopped parsley

- Cut squash in half, remove seeds and steam 1/2 squash until just tender.
- Mix soy sauce, seasoning and water chestnuts with rice and place in the center of the squash.
- Place stuffed squash in pie plate with 1/2 inch water.
- Bake in oven preheated to 350 for 30 minutes.
- Sprinkle parsley on top.

Yield: about 2 cups squash with rice.
One serving: 1/2 cup.

Per serving:

calories	238
protein	5.9 grams
fat	2.2 grams
carbohydrate	50.7 grams
fiber	4.0 grams
cholesterol	0 milligrams
sodium	48 milligrams

Diabetes exchanges:

2 starch
2 vegetable

SERVING SUGGESTION:

Place two tablespoons of crushed pineapple (with no sugar added) in the center of the squash before you add the rice.

LASAGNA

4 lasagna noodles (whole wheat preferred, no cholesterol, no sodium), cooked according to directions on package

1 cup TOMATO PURÉE (p. 69)

1 cup chopped spinach, steamed

4 ounces hoop cheese crumbled

1 medium onion, chopped

2 teaspoons olive oil

1 teaspoon SALT FREE SEASONING (p. 51), or 1/4 teaspoon each of basil, oregano, garlic powder and onion powder and 1/8 teaspoon pepper.

- Layer ingredients in lightly greased loaf pan (about 8 by 5 by 2-1/2 inches).
- Bake in oven preheated to 350 degrees for about 45 minutes.

Yield: 4 portions. One serving: 1/4 loaf pan.

Per serving:

calories 175
protein . . . . 10.8 grams
fat . . . . 3.2 grams
carbohydrate . . . . 29.0 grams
fiber . . . . 5.7 grams
cholesterol . . . . 2 milligrams
sodium . . . . 40 milligrams

Diabetes exchanges:

1-1/2 starch
1 lean meat/fish
1 vegetable

FOR VARIETY:

Use any green leafy vegetable, such as chard or kale, instead of spinach.

LENTILS

1/2 cup lentils

1-1/2 cup water

pinch of salt (less than 1/8 teaspoon, optional, add 72 milligrams sodium per serving)

- **Boil water, add lentils, and simmer for 15 minutes, or until lentils are tender but not mushy.**

Yield: 1 cup. One serving: 1/2 cup.

Per serving:

calories	162
protein	13.5 grams
fat	0.5 grams
carbohydrate	27.4 grams
fiber	5.5 grams
cholesterol	0 milligrams
sodium	5 milligrams

Diabetes exchanges:

2 starch
1 lean meat/fish

LENTIL AND BROWN RICE LOAF

1 cup cooked LENTILS (p. 137)

1 cup cooked BROWN RICE (p. 152)

1/2 cup chopped onions

1/2 cup unfiltered apple juice

1 teaspoon curry powder (or 1/2 teaspoon each of oregano and basil)

1/2 teaspoon cumin (or 1/2 teaspoon thyme)

1/2 teaspoon dry mustard

1/2 teaspoon garlic powder

1 egg white, slightly beaaten

- Combine lentils, brown rice and onions.
- Add apple juice, curry powder, cumin, mustard and garlic powder.
- Mix in egg white and place in lightly greased loaf pan (about 9 by 5 by 2-1/2 inches).
- Bake in oven preheated to 350 degrees for about 50 minutes.

Yield: 1 loaf. One serving: 1/4 loaf.

Per serving:

calories 143
protein . . . . 7.1 grams
fat . . . . 0.9 grams
carbohydrate . . . . 27.4 grams
fiber . . . . 3.4 grams
cholesterol . . . . 0 milligrams
sodium . . . . 19 milligrams

Diabetes exchanges:

2 starch

LOW VISION TIP #14:

Wearing glasses while cooking protects your eyes. If you do not have a prescription pair good for the distance needed in cooking, wear clear glasses.

MANICOTTI

6 pieces of manicotti, no cholesterol and no sodium*

4 ounces unsalted hoop cheese

1 tablespoon non-fat plain yogurt

3/4 cup chopped spinach (or another green leafy vegetable)

1 tablespoon lemon juice

1/2 cup plum tomatoes, cut up

1 teaspoon olive oil

1 teaspoon canola oil

1 teaspoon SALT FREE SEASONING (p. 51), or 1/4 teaspoon each of oregano, basil, onion powder and garlic powder and 1/8 teaspoon pepper.

3/4 cup TOMATO SAUCE (p. 68)

- Cook manicotti according to directions on package.
- Prepare stuffing while manicotti is boiling.
- Mix hoop cheese with non-fat yogurt, spinach, lemon juice, tomatoes, olive and canola oils and seasoning.
- Stuff manicotti when they are boiled and rinsed.
- Place in lightly greased pan (about 8 by 8 inches) and cover with tomato sauce.

- Bake in oven preheated to 350 degrees for about 30 minutes.

Yield: 6 manicotti. One serving: 1 manicotti.

Per serving:

calories 101
protein . . . . 6.4 grams
fat . . . . 2.1 grams
carbohydrate . . . . 16.0 grams
fiber . . . . 3.0 grams
cholesterol . . . . 1 milligram
sodium . . . . 25 milligrams

Diabetes exchanges:

1 starch
1 lean meat/fish

*If you want to use only whole grain products, you may substitute whole wheat chapati for the manicotti. Place the stuffing inside chapati and bake for 20 minutes in oven preheated to 350 degrees.

MATZO APPLE PUDDING

2 cups matzo farfel (matzos broken into small pieces, whole wheat preferred)

1 cup cored, peeled, and sliced apples

1/2 cup unfiltered apple juice

1/2 ounce raisins

1-1/2 teaspoons cinnamon

1/8 teaspoon salt (optional, 48 milligrams sodium per serving)

3 egg whites, beaten but not stiff

- Soak matzo farfel in warm water for 10 minutes, place in a colander and squeeze out excess water.
- Combine farfel with apples, apple juice, raisins, cinnamon and salt (if used).
- Fold in egg whites.
- Pour mixture into lightly greased baking dish (about 8 inches square).
- Bake in oven preheated to 350 degrees, or until a knife inserted into the center comes out dry. Be careful not to overbake or the pudding will be dry.

Yield: 6 pieces about 4 inches square.
One serving: 1 piece.

Calculations are based on whole wheat matzos.

Per serving:

calories 96
protein . . . . 3.8 grams
fat . . . . 0.8 grams
carbohydrate . . . . 19.6 grams
fiber . . . . 1.4 grams
cholesterol . . . . 0 milligrams
sodium . . . . 33 milligrams

Diabetes exchanges:

1 starch

SERVING SUGGESTION:

An excellent part of a holiday meal plan.

NOODLE-APPLE KUGEL

1 package medium (12 ounces) noodles (preferably whole wheat, no cholesterol or sodium)

2 apples, peeled, cored, and sliced thinly

2 tablespoons cinnamon

1 tablespoon vanilla

2 tablespoons raisins (1/4 cup)

1/4 teaspoon salt (optional, add 48 milligrams sodium per serving)

3/4 cup unfiltered apple juice

4 egg whites, beaten moderately

1 egg

- Boil noodles in 2 quarts water until tender, but not overcooked (about 10 minutes).

- Drain noodles in colander and rinse with cold water.

- Stir together noodles, apple slices, cinnamon, vanilla, raisins and salt (if used) and apple juice.

- Mix egg with egg whites and fold into mixture.

- Place in lightly greased pan about 8 by 11 inches.

- Bake in oven preheated to 350 degrees for about 20 minutes, cover with aluminum foil, and bake for an additional 15 minutes.

Yield: about 12 pieces. One serving: 1 piece.

Per serving:

calories 141
protein . . . . 5.9 grams
fat . . . . 1.0 grams
carbohydrate . . . . 28.9 grams
fiber . . . . 4.3 grams
cholesterol . . . . 18 milligrams
sodium . . . . 24 milligrams

Diabetes exchanges:

2 starch

SERVING SUGGESTION:

Serve for holiday meals. Extra portions may be frozen and used later.

PASTA WITH KALE

2 cups cooked linguini, preferably whole wheat, no cholesterol and no sodium

1/2 cup TOMATO PURÉE (p. 69)

2 medium plum tomatoes (or 1 medium tomato), chopped

1/4 cup chopped onions

1/4 cup chopped apple

1 teaspoon olive oil

3/4 teaspoon SALT FREE SEASONING (p. 51), or 1/4 teaspoon each of oregano, basil and thyme and 1/8 teaspoon pepper

1 cup kale, broken into pieces, stems removed

- Cook pasta according to directions on package.
- Combine puréed tomatoes, tomatoes, onions, apple, olive oil and seasoning.
- Layer linguini, puréed tomato mixture and kale in lightly greased baking dish (about 8 by 8 inches).
- Bake in oven preheated to 350 degrees for 30 minutes.

Yield: 4 portions. One serving: 1/4 pasta in baking dish.

Per serving:

calories 170
protein . . . . 7.3 grams
fat . . . . 2.1 grams
carbohydrate . . . . 38.1 grams
fiber . . . . 6.3 grams
cholesterol . . . . 0 milligrams
sodium . . . . 12 milligrams

Diabetes exchanges:

2 starch

FOR VARIETY:

Use any green leafy vegetable, such as spinach or chard, instead of kale.

POTATO KUGEL

2 cups grated baking potatoes

1/3 cup grated onions

3 egg whites

1/8 teaspoon freshly ground black pepper (or to taste)

- Mix grated potatoes and onions together.
- Add egg whites and pepper and mix quickly.
- Place kugel into lightly greased pan (9 inch pie plate or 8 by 8 by 2 inch rectangular pan).
- Preheat oven to 350 degrees and bake for 40 minutes, or until kugel is browned.

Yield: 1 kugel. One serving: 1/4 of kugel.

Per serving:

calories	87
protein	4.1 grams
fat	0.1 grams
carbohydrate	17.6 grams
fiber	1.5 grams
cholesterol	0 milligrams
sodium	44 milligrams

1 starch

FOR VARIETY:

As an alternative, you may substitute 2 cups of mashed, steamed or baked potatoes for the grated potatoes.

POTATO MARBLES:

Roll mixture into balls about 1-2 inches in diameter. Place on a lightly greased cookie sheet. Preheat oven to 350 degrees and bake until browned, about 20 minutes. Turn and complete baking in about 10 minutes. Yield: about 24 marbles. One serving: 6 marbles.

RATATOUILLE

1 medium eggplant, cut into 1 inch cubes

2 medium zucchini, cut into 1 inch cubes

1/2 sweet pepper (red, green, yellow or a mix), cut into small pieces

1 onion, sliced

1 cup plum tomatoes, cut into 1 inch pieces

2 teaspoons olive oil

1 teaspoon SALT FREE SEASONING (p. 51), or 1/4 teaspoon each of oregano, basil, garlic powder and ginger and 1/8 teaspoon pepper

* Mix all vegetables together.
* Stir in olive oil and seasoning.
* Place mixture in casserole, cover and cook for 35 minutes in oven preheated to 350 degrees.
* If the ratatouille appears to have too much liquid, remove casserole lid.
* Continue cooking for an additional 15 minutes.

Yield: about 4 cups vegetables.
One serving: 1 cup.

Per serving:

calories 78
protein . . . . 2.6 grams
fat . . . . 2.7 grams
carbohydrate . . . . 13.3 grams
fiber . . . . 3.0 grams
cholesterol . . . . 0 milligrams
sodium . . . . 11 milligrams

Diabetes exchanges:

2 vegetable
1/2 fat

SERVING SUGGESTION:

Makes enough for 2 days. The second day it may taste even better than the first, since the flavors have more time to blend.

BROWN RICE

3/4 cup brown rice, either long grain or short grain*

1-1/2 cups water

1/8 teaspoon salt (optional, add 72 milligrams sodium per serving)

- Place ingredients in a medium saucepan.
- Bring to a boil and reduce heat.
- Simmer covered for about 45 minutes.
- Fluff rice with a fork.

Yield: about 2 cups rice. One serving: 1/2 cup.

Per serving:

calories	128
protein	2.8 grams
fat	1.0 grams
carbohydrate	26.8 grams
fiber	1.2 grams
cholesterol	0 milligrams
sodium	2 milligrams

Diabetes exchanges:

1-1/2 starch

*For variety: Use BASMATI RICE or WILD RICE instead of BROWN RICE. Combine 1/4 cup WILD RICE with 3/4 cup BROWN RICE.

TABOULI

1/2 cup bulgur wheat

1 cup boiling water

1/4 cup chopped parsley

1/8 cup chopped scallions, with greens

1 clove garlic, minced

2 tablespoons lemon juice

1 teaspoon unseasoned rice vinegar

pinch of salt (less than 1/8 teaspoon, optional, add 48 milligrams sodium per serving)

1/8 teaspoon pepper or to taste

- Place wheat in a bowl and pour boiling water over it.
- Leave in the bowl for about 30 minutes and squeeze out excess water.
- Add the rest of the ingredients and place in the refrigerator until ready to serve.

Yield: 1-1/2 cups. One serving: 1/2 cup.

Per serving:

calories	33
protein	1.2 grams
fat	0.1 grams
carbohydrate	7.6 grams
fiber	0.4 grams
cholesterol	0 milligrams
sodium	4 milligrams

Diabetes exchanges:

1/2 starch

SERVING SUGGESTION:

Use as hor d'oeuvres with crackers.

TOFU-PASTA-VEGETABLE COMBO

2 cups whole wheat spiral pasta, no cholesterol and no sodium

1 cup broccoli flowerettes

1 medium onion

1 medium zucchini

1 crooked neck or patty pan summer squash

1 medium carrot

1 cup quartered plum tomatoes

1-1/2 teaspoons SALT FREE SEASONING (p. 51), or 1/4 teaspoon each of thyme, basil, oregano and ginger and 1/8 teaspoon pepper

1/4 cup unfiltered apple juice

1 tablespoon lemon juice

2 ounces low sodium, low fat tofu cheese*

- Boil pasta until *al dente* (slightly underdone) and drain in a colander.
- Steam broccoli, onion, squash and carrot. The onion, broccoli and carrot will take longer to steam than the zucchini. Do not overcook.
- Add steamed vegetables to pasta.
- Add tomatoes, seasoning and apple and lemon juices.
- Place in lightly greased baking dish.

- Grate or cut up tofu cheese on top of pasta and bake for 25 minutes in oven preheated to 300 degrees.

Yield: 6 cups. One serving: 3/4 cup.

Per serving:

calories	132
protein	7.0 grams
fat	1.9 grams
carbohydrate	27.1 grams
fiber	4.8 grams
cholesterol	0 milligrams
sodium	23 milligrams

Diabetes exchanges:

1-1/2 starch
1/2 lean meat/fish
2 vegetable

*If you cannot find low fat, low sodium tofu cheese, substitute plain tofu.

LOW VISION TIP #15:

When steaming vegetables, tip the pot slightly to feel the weight of the water. In this way, you can tell whether there is enough water in the pot.

TOFU STIR FRY

6 ounces tofu, cut into 1 inch cubes

2 teaspoons canola oil

1/4 cup unfiltered apple juice

1/4 cup water

1/4 cup of each vegetable, thinly sliced: carrots, potatoes, zucchini, mushrooms, onions, celery, cabbage, sweet pepper and leek (total of 2-1/4 cups)

1/4 cup China peas

1/4 cup string beans, cut into 1 inch pieces

1/2 teaspoon grated ginger

1/2 cup broccoli, broken into small pieces

1 teaspoon SALT FREE SEASONING (p. 51) or 1/4 teaspoon each of oregano, basil, thyme, mustard, and 1/8 teaspoon pepper

1 teaspoon low sodium soy sauce

1/2 cup water chestnuts, thinly sliced

1/2 cup bean sprouts

- Add canola oil, a little apple juice and a little water to wok or large skillet.
- Stir fry tofu, vegetables, seasoning, ginger and soy sauce.

- Water chestnuts and bean sprouts take less time than the other vegetables, so add them last.
- Add remaining apple juice and water as needed.

Yield: 6 cups. One serving: 1 cup.

Per serving:

calories	66
protein	3.9 grams
fat	3.1 grams
carbohydrate	7.1 grams
fiber	1.8 grams
cholesterol	0 milligrams
sodium	44 milligrams

Diabetes exchanges:

1 vegetable
1/2 medium fat

VEGETARIAN TOSTADA

4 corn tortillas, no salt added, 6 inches in diameter
1/2 cup cooked BEANS (p. 114)
1/2 cup cooked BROWN RICE (p. 152)
1/4 cup chopped onions
1/4 cup chopped tomatoes
1/4 teaspoon cumin
1/4 teaspoon chili powder
1/4 teaspoon dry mustard
1/8 teaspoon pepper or to taste
1/2 cup plain non-fat yogurt
4-6 leaves of lettuce
2 sprigs of watercress

- Warm tortillas in oven or microwave.
- Mix onions and tomatoes and 1/2 of seasoning with beans.
- Mix the other 1/2 of seasoning with rice.
- Place a scoop of beans and rice on each tortilla and put a scoop of yogurt on top.
- Garnish with lettuce and watercress.

Yield: 4 tostadas. One serving: 1 tostada.

Per serving:

calories	154
protein	6.8 grams
fat	1.7 grams
carbohydrate	28.8 grams
fiber	3.2 grams
cholesterol	1 milligram
sodium	28 milligrams

Diabetes exchanges:

2 starch

FOR VARIETY:

Use chapati instead of tortillas. Fill each chapati with mixture and bake in an oven preheated to 325 degrees for 30 minutes.

YAMS AND APPLES

3 medium yams
2 apples (golden delicious, or pippin)
1/2 cup unfiltered apple juice
juice of 2 lemons

* Wash and cut yams in 3 inch pieces.
* Steam until yams may be pierced with a fork (tender, but firm).*
* Plunge steamed yams into a bowl of cold water.
* Remove the skins, and cut off 1/2 inch from each end piece to remove fibrous material.
* Sprinkle yams with lemon juice.
* Peel and cut apples into 1 to 2 inch pieces.
* Place apples and apple juice in a medium sized pot.
* Cook over medium heat until apples are tender but firm.
* Sprinkle apples with lemon juice.
* Combine yams and apples.
* If not eaten right away, the mixture may be refrigerated and reheated later. Often, the flavor improves if the mixture is prepared in advance.

As an alternative, bake the yams and peel.

Per serving:

calories	149
protein	1.5 grams
fat	0.3 grams
carbohydrate	36.6 grams
fiber	1.3 grams
cholesterol	0 milligrams
sodium	8 milligrams

Diabetes exchanges:

1 starch
1-1/2 fruit

<table>
<tr>
<td>

FOR VARIETY:

Purée the mixture in a food processor. Do not over process. Heat and serve.

</td>
<td>

SERVING SUGGESTION:

Good for holiday meals, such as Thanksgiving and Hannukah.

</td>
</tr>
</table>

ZUCCHINI AND WATER CHESTNUTS

2 cups zucchini (about 2-3 zucchini), sliced
1 medium onion, sliced
1/2 cup SALSA (p. 66)
3 plum tomatoes, quartered
1/2 cup water chestnuts

- Steam zucchini and onions separately until slightly underdone. The onions will take a little more time.
- Combine SALSA with plum tomatoes, place in a pot and simmer over medium heat for 5 minutes.
- Add zucchini, onion, SALSA, tomatoes and water chestnuts and simmer for an additional 5 minutes over medium heat.

Yield: about 2 cups. One serving: 1/2 cup.

Per serving:

calories 39
protein . . . . 1.5 grams
fat . . . . 0.3 grams
carbohydrate . . . . 7.5 grams
fiber . . . . 0.9 grams
cholesterol . . . . 0 milligrams
sodium . . . . 7 milligrams

Diabetes exchanges:

1 vegetable

FOR VARIETY:

*Add slivered almonds or steamed
sliced onions.*

CHAPTER 6

MUFFINS, QUICK BREADS, YEAST BREADS AND CRACKERS

MUFFINS

APRICOT MUFFINS

2 cups whole wheat flour (preferably stone ground)

2 teaspoons baking powder (non-aluminum)

1/2 teaspoon cinnamon

1/2 teaspoon allspice

1/2 cup apricot juice (from fruit or can, no sugar added)

1/2 cup unfiltered apple juice

1/2 teaspoon vanilla

2 teaspoons canola oil

1/2 cup apricots, cut into pieces (about 3 apricots)

- Combine dry ingredients.
- Mix vanilla with apricot and apple juices and add to mixture.
- Add canola oil and apricots.
- Lightly grease non-stick muffin pan and fill 3/4 full.
- Bake in oven preheated to 350 degrees for 15 minutes, or until knife inserted in center of a muffin comes out dry.

Yield: 12 muffins. One serving: 1 muffin.

calories	90
protein	2.9 grams
fat	1.2 grams
carbohydrate	18.2 grams
fiber	2.7 grams
cholesterol	0 milligrams
sodium	52 milligrams

Diabetes exchanges:

1 starch

FOR VARIETY—PRUNE MUFFINS:

*Substitute 1/2 cup cut up prunes
for the apricots.*

BANANA NUT MUFFINS

1 cup whole wheat flour (preferably stone ground)

1 cup oat bran

2 teaspoons baking powder (non-aluminum)

1 teaspoon allspice

1 cup unfiltered apple juice

1/2 cup mashed banana

1 teaspoon vanilla

2 teaspoons canola oil

2 tablespoons chopped walnuts

- Combine dry ingredients.
- Add apple juice, banana, vanilla, canola oil and nuts.
- Spoon mixture into lightly greased muffin pan.
- Bake for 15 minutes in oven preheated to 350 degrees.

Yield: 12 muffins. One serving: 1 muffin.

Per serving:

calories 88
protein . . . . 3.0 grams
fat . . . . 2.3 grams
carbohydrate . . . . 17.4 grams
fiber . . . . 2.8 grams
cholesterol . . . . 0 milligrams
sodium . . . . 5.2 milligrams

Diabetes exchanges:

1 starch

LOW VISION TIP #16:

Some find it helpful to fill a muffin pan by scooping the mixture with an ice cream scoop.

WHOLE WHEAT BLUEBERRY MUFFINS

2 cups whole wheat flour (preferably stone ground)

2 teaspoons baking powder (non-aluminum)

1 teaspoon cinnamon

1-1/4 cups unfiltered apple juice

1-1/2 teaspoon vanilla

2 teaspoons canola oil

1-1/2 cup frozen blueberries (no sugar added)

- Combine dry ingredients.
- Stir vanilla in apple juice and add to dry ingredients.
- Add canola oil and gently fold in blueberries.
- Spoon into lightly greased muffin pan.
- Bake in oven preheated to 350 degrees for 15 minutes, or until knife inserted in the center of a muffin comes out dry.

Yield: 12 muffins. One serving: 1 muffin.

Per serving:

calories 100
protein . . . . 2.8 grams
fat . . . . 1.3 grams
carbohydrate . . . . 20.6 grams
fiber . . . . 3.3 grams
cholesterol . . . . 0 milligrams
sodium . . . . 52 milligrams

Diabetes exchanges:

1 starch

PLEASE REMEMBER:

If you eat 2 muffins, double the calories and other items in the nutritional analysis.

CORN MUFFINS

1-1/2 cups corn meal

1/2 cup whole wheat flour (preferably stone ground)

2 teaspoons baking powder (non-aluminum)

1/8 teaspoon salt (optional, add 24 milligrams sodium per serving)

1 cup unfiltered apple juice

1/2 cup thick applesauce

2 teaspoons canola oil

- Combine dry ingredients.
- Add apple juice, applesauce and canola oil.
- Spoon into lightly greased muffin pan.
- Place in oven preheated to 350 degrees and bake for about 10-12 minutes or until knife inserted in the center of a muffin comes out dry.

Yield: 12 muffins. One serving: 1 muffin.

FOR VARIETY:

Add 1/4 cup grated onions and 1/4 cup grated red, yellow, green or purple sweet peppers.

DATE-BRAN MUFFINS

3/4 cup whole wheat flour (preferably stone ground)

3/4 cup oat bran

3/4 cup wheat bran

2 teaspoons baking powder (non-aluminum)

1-1/2 teaspoons cinnamon

1 cup unfiltered apple juice

2 teaspoons vanilla

2 teaspoons canola oil

1/4 cup dates, cut into small pieces and mixed with 1 tablespoon flour

---

- Combine dry ingredients.
- Add vanilla to apple juice and mix with dry ingredients.
- Mix in canola oil and dates.
- Bake in oven preheated to 350 degrees for about 10-12 minutes, or until knife inserted in the center of a muffin comes out clean.

Yield: 12 muffins. One serving: 1 muffin.

Per serving:

calories 80
protein . . . . 3.7 grams
fat . . . . 2.0 grams
carbohydrate . . . . 17.9 grams
fiber . . . . 5.3 grams
cholesterol . . . . 0 milligrams
sodium . . . . 52 milligrams

Diabetes exchanges:

1 starch

SERVING SUGGESTION:

Excellent for lunch or as a between main meal snack.

OAT BRAN-WHEAT MUFFINS

1 cup oat bran

1 cup whole wheat flour (preferably stone ground)

2 teaspoons baking powder (non-aluminum)

1/2 teaspoon cinnamon

1/2 teaspoon allspice

1 cup unfiltered apple juice

1/2 teaspoon vanilla

2 teaspoons canola oil

1/2 ounce raisins

- Combine dry ingredients.
- Mix vanilla into apple juice and add to mixture.
- Add canola oil and raisins.
- Lightly oil non-stick muffin pan and fill 3/4 full.
- Bake in oven preheated to 350 degrees for 15 minutes, or until knife inserted in the center of a muffin comes out dry.

Yield: 12 muffins. One serving: 1 muffin

calories	74
protein	2.8 grams
fat	1.5 grams
carbohydrate	16.0 grams
fiber	2.6 grams
cholesterol	0 milligrams
sodium	52 milligrams

Diabetes exchanges:

1 starch

FOR VARIETY:

Use 2 cups of oat bran instead of the combination of oat bran and wheat.

Instead of raisins, you can add thinly sliced pieces of apple or thinly sliced pieces of 1 small banana.

PUMPKIN MUFFINS

1-1/4 cups whole wheat flour (preferably stone ground)

1-1/2 teaspoon baking powder (non-aluminum)

1/2 teaspoon cinnamon

1/4 teaspoon nutmeg

1/3 teaspoon ginger

3/4 cup unfiltered apple juice

1 teaspoon vanilla

1/2 cup pumpkin purée

1/2 ounce raisins

2 teaspoons canola oil

- Combine dry ingredients.
- Add vanilla to apple juice and stir into mixture.
- Mix in pumpkin purée, raisins, and canola oil.
- Pour into lightly greased muffin pan.
- Bake in oven preheated to 350 degrees for 15 minutes or until a knife inserted in the center of a muffin comes out dry.

Yield: 9 muffins. One serving: 1 muffin.

Per serving:

calories	88
protein	2.5 grams
fat	1.4 grams
carbohydrate	17.3 grams
fiber	2.5 grams
cholesterol	0 milligrams
sodium	52 milligrams

Diabetes exchanges:

1 starch

FOR VARIETY:

Use puréed kabocha or butternut squash instead of pumpkin.

QUICK BREADS

BANANA BREAD

2 cups whole wheat flour (preferably stone ground)

1/2 cup oat bran

1/4 cup wheat bran

3 teaspoons baking powder (non-aluminum)

1 teaspoon cinnamon

1 teaspoon cloves

1 teaspoon allspice

1 tablespoon vanilla

1 tablespoon lemon juice

1-1/2 cups unfiltered apple juice

1-1/2 cups mashed, somewhat lumpy ripe bananas

2 teaspoons canola oil

3 egg whites, beaten but not stiff

* Combine dry ingredients.
* Stir vanilla and lemon juice in apple juice and add to dry ingredients.
* Mix in mashed bananas and canola oil.
* Fold in egg whites.
* Pour mixture into lightly greased loaf pan (about 8 by 5 by 2-1/2 inches).

- Bake in oven preheated to 350 degrees for about 50 to 60 minutes, or until a knife inserted into the center comes out dry.

Yield: 16 half inch slices. One serving: 1 piece.

Per serving:

calories	103
protein	3.6 grams
fat	1.3 grams
carbohydrate	21.8 grams
fiber	3.2 grams
cholesterol	0 milligrams
sodium	68 milligrams

Diabetes exchanges:

1-1/2 starch

LOW VISION TIP #17:

Use an egg separator to remove the whites.

ZUCCHINI-ONION CORN BREAD

1-1/2 cups corn meal

1/2 cup oat bran

2 teaspoons baking powder (non-aluminum)

1 cup grated zucchini

1/4 cup chopped onions

1-1/2 teaspoons SALT FREE SEASONING (p. 51)

1 cup unfiltered apple juice

2 teaspoons canola oil

2 egg whites, beaten moderately

* Mix corn meal, oat bran and baking powder.
* In a separate bowl, mix zucchini, onions, and seasoning.
* Add zucchini mixture to the flour mixture alternately with apple juice.
* Add canola oil and fold in egg whites.
* Place in lightly greased loaf pan (about 8 by 5 by 2 1/2 inches).
* Bake in oven preheated to 350 degrees for about 50 minutes, or until knife inserted in center comes out dry.

Yield: 16 pieces. One serving: 1 piece.

Per serving:

calories	87
protein	2.2 grams
fat	1.0 grams
carbohydrate	17 grams
fiber	1.2 grams
cholesterol	0 milligrams
sodium	61 milligrams

Diabetes exchanges:

1 starch

FOR VARIETY:

Add 1/2 cup grated apples with peels.

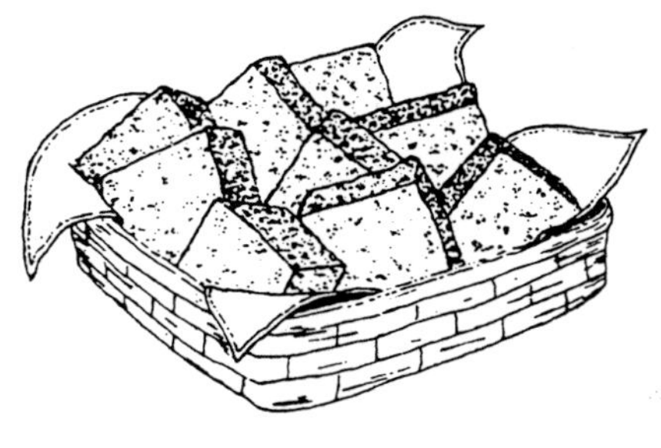

YEAST BREADS AND CRACKERS

WHOLE WHEAT BREAD

2-3/4 cups whole wheat flour (preferably stone ground)

1/4 teaspoon salt (optional, add 48 milligrams sodium per serving)

3 tablespoons warm water

1 tablespoons active dry yeast

1 cup non-fat milk

1 teaspoon canola oil

2 tablespoons raisins simmered in 3 tablespoons water

- Warm flour for 10 minutes in oven set at 200 degrees.

- Put 3 tablespoons of warm water in a small bowl, add yeast and let this sit until bubbles form. (If they do not form, get another package of yeast and start over).

- Place raisins in a strainer and press with a spoon to extract the juice (about 2 tablespoons).

- In a small saucepan, warm milk, oil, salt and raisin juice. These liquids should be lukewarm (between 105 to 115 degrees). If it is warmer, it will make the yeast too bubbly or will destroy its action. If it is too cool, the yeast will not raise the dough efficiently.

- Add the bubbling yeast to the liquids and mix in half the flour.
- Add the remaining flour and mix until the dough forms a ball.
- Set the dough on a floured bread board and knead until the dough is elastic and not sticky. If you use a food processor with a dough hook, this step should take only 5 minutes.
- Place the dough in a lightly greased bowl, cover with a dish towel, and set it in a warm location (around 80 to 85 degrees) such as an oven or a warm kitchen.
- When the dough has doubled in bulk, set it on a floured bread board, punch it down and knead a few times.
- Place it in the bowl again, cover with a towel and let it double again.
- Set the dough on the bread board, punch it down and shape it into a loaf.
- Place in a lightly greased loaf pan (about 8 by 5 by 2-1/2 inches) and when doubled in bulk bake for about 45 minutes in oven preheated to 350 degrees.

Yield: one loaf, about 12 slices.
One serving: 1 slice.

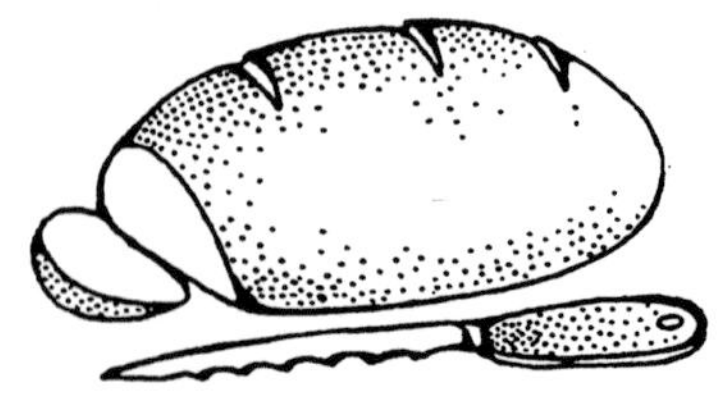

Per serving:

calories 108
protein . . . . 4.8 grams
fat . . . . 0.9 grams
carbohydrate . . . . 22.4 grams
fiber . . . . 3.8 grams
cholesterol . . . . 0 milligrams
sodium . . . . 13 milligrams

Diabetes exchanges:

1-1/2 starch

LOW VISION TIP #18:

The most frequently used temperature setting of your oven may be marked with Hi Mark. This provides a raised material so you can feel the correct setting. Usually 350 degrees is marked. Ask the low vision center in your region where to buy the marker.

WHOLE WHEAT ROLLS

Dough from WHOLE WHEAT BREAD recipe
(p. 187)

1 tablespoon sesame seeds

- Prepare dough the same as for WHOLE WHEAT BREAD.
- After second rising, shape dough into 12 rolls (either round or twisted).
- Dip top into sesame seeds.
- Place on a lightly greased cookie sheet and let rise until double in bulk.
- Place in oven preheated to 325 degrees and bake for about 10 to 15 minutes.

Yield: 12 rolls. One serving: 1 roll.

Per serving:

calories	108
protein	4.8 grams
fat	0.9 grams
carbohydrate	22.4 grams
fiber	3.8 grams
cholesterol	0 milligrams
sodium	13 milligrams

Diabetes exchanges:

1-1/2 starch

WHOLE WHEAT PITA BREAD

Dough from WHOLE WHEAT BREAD recipe (p. 187)

- After second rising of dough, divide into 12 balls.

- Roll out each one on a floured bread board. They should measure around 1/4 inch thick and 6 to 7 inches in diameter.

- Place the pita on a lightly greased cookie sheet and bake them for 5 to 10 minutes in hot oven preheated to 425 degrees.

Yield: 12 pieces. One serving: 1 pita bread.

Per serving:

calories	108
protein	4.8 grams
fat	0.9 grams
carbohydrate	22.4 grams
fiber	3.8 grams
cholesterol	0 milligrams
sodium	13 milligrams

Diabetes exchanges:

1-1/2 starch

FOR VARIETY:

Substitute water for milk.

WHOLE WHEAT FRENCH BREAD

1-1/2 cups whole wheat flour (preferably stone ground)

1-1/2 cups whole wheat pastry flour (preferably stone ground)

1/4 teaspoon salt (optional, add 32 milligrams sodium per serving)

1-1/4 cup water

1-1/2 teaspoon active dry yeast

1 tablespoon corn meal

- Combine flour and salt (if used).
- Place yeast in 1/4 cup warm water and let stand for 5-10 minutes.
- Combine flour mixture with yeast and water and remaining water.
- Using a floured bread board, knead until dough is a good consistency. If it seems too sticky, add a little more flour. The dough should feel bouncy and come back into shape when you press it with your finger. You may use a food processor with a dough hook.
- Place the dough in a lightly greased bowl, cover with a towel, and let stand until double in bulk.

- Punch down, knead a few times, and shape into
  a loaf.
- Place the corn meal on the bread board and
  press the bottom of the loaf on the meal.
- Set the loaf on a lightly greased cookie sheet
  and cover with a towel.
- After it has doubled in bulk, cut diagonal lines
  across the top of the loaf (about 1/2 inch deep
  and about 2 inches apart).
- Place in oven preheated to 400 degrees and
  bake for about 25 minutes.

Yield: one loaf, 18 slices. One serving: 1 slice.

Per serving:

calories	70
protein	2.9 grams
fat	0.4 grams
carbohydrate	15.0 grams
fiber	2.6 grams
cholesterol	0 milligrams
sodium	1 milligram

Diabetes exchanges:

1 starch

NOTE:

100% whole wheat flour will make a dense, but tasty loaf.

If you wish a lighter loaf, try 1-1/2 cups whole wheat pastry flour and 1-1/2 cups unbleached white flour.

FOR VARIETY:

Substitute 1/2 cup non-fat plain yogurt for 1/2 cup water (still use 3/4 cup water). This recipe tastes more like sourdough bread.

WHOLE WHEAT FRENCH ROLLS

Dough from WHOLE WHEAT FRENCH BREAD
recipe (p. 192)

* Shape the dough into 18 rolls, either round or
  elongated.
* Bake in oven preheated to 325 degrees for
  about 15 minutes.

Yield: 18 rolls. One serving: 1 roll.

Per serving:

calories	70
protein	2.9 grams
fat	0.4 grams
carbohydrate	15.0 grams
fiber	2.6 grams
cholesterol	0 milligrams
sodium	1 milligram

Diabetes exchanges:

1 starch

WHOLE WHEAT SESAME CRACKERS

1/2 cup plus 2 tablespoons warm water

1 tablespoon active dry yeast

1-1/2 cups whole wheat pastry flour (preferably stone ground)

1/4 teaspoon salt (optional, add 38 milligrams sodium per serving)

1 tablespoon canola oil

2 tablespoons unfiltered apple juice

2 teaspoons sesame seeds

* Sprinkle yeast in warm water and let stand for 10 minutes.
* Combine flour and salt (if used).
* Mix flour with yeast and water, oil and apple juice.
* Shape into a ball and place mixture in a lightly greased bowl.
* Cover and let stand for 30 minutes.
* On a floured bread board roll out dough to 1/8 inch thick.
* Sprinkle with sesame seeds and roll again.
* Place rolled out dough on lightly greased cookie sheet (you may need two).

- Cut into squares, triangles or use a cookie cutter.
- Place in oven preheated to 350 degrees and bake until crisp for about 12 to 15 minutes.

Yield: about 30 crackers. One serving: 2 crackers.

Per serving:

calories	53
protein	1.9 grams
fat	1.3 grams
carbohydrate	9.3 grams
fiber	1.7 grams
cholesterol	0 milligrams
sodium	1 milligram

Diabetes exchanges:

1/2 starch

LOW VISION TIP #19:

Tap cracker with a wooden spoon or your fingernail to test for crispness.

CHAPTER 7

CREPES, CEREALS AND PANCAKES

CREPES

CREPES

1 cup whole wheat pastry flour (preferably stone ground)
1-1/4 cups non-fat milk
1 medium egg
2 egg whites

- Mix ingredients together and place in blender or food processor for a short time to eliminate lumps.
- Set in the refrigerator for 1 hour.
- Heat non-stick skillet measuring 6 inches in diameter at the bottom.
- Set burner on medium heat, or just below.
- Pour about 2-3 tablespoons of mixture onto the pan and tip pan to cover the bottom with mixture. Pour off excess.
- Let crepes cook a few minutes until edges loosen easily with a knife.
- Remove the crepes and place on a kitchen towel, bottom side up.

Yield: 16 crepes. One serving: 1 crepe.

Per serving:

calories 38
protein . . . . 2.4 grams
fat . . . . 0.4 grams
carbohydrate . . . . 6.4 grams
fiber . . . . 0.9 grams
cholesterol . . . . 11.8 milligrams
sodium . . . . 20 milligrams

Diabetes exchanges:

1/2 starch

SERVING SUGGESTION:

You may freeze extra crepes. Place waxed paper between each crepe and cover stack with tightly wrapped freezer paper or a zipped plastic bag.

APPLE BLINTZES

4 medium apples, cored, peeled, and cut into eighths

1/2 teaspoon cinnamon

1/4 cup unfiltered apple juice

1 tablespoon lemon juice

6 CREPES (p. 201)

- Place apples in saucepan and sprinkle with lemon juice and cinnamon.
- Add apple juice and cook over medium heat until apples are slightly underdone (test with a fork).
- Place a heaping tablespoon of apples on crepe, fold ends and sides, and set in lightly greased skillet.
- Cover and cook over medium heat for about 15 minutes, or until browned.
- Turn and cook another 5 minutes.

Yield: 6 blintzes. One serving: 1 blintz.

Per serving:

calories	94
protein	2.7 grams
fat	0.8 grams
carbohydrate	20.7 grams
fiber	3.3 grams
cholesterol	14 milligrams
sodium	21 milligrams

Diabetes exchanges:

1 starch
1/2 fruit

FOR VARIETY:

Make BLUEBERRY BLINTZES with fresh or frozen blueberries.

Make PRUNE BLINTZES with cooked and mashed prunes.

CHEESE BLINTZES

4 ounces unsalted hoop cheese

1/4 cup plain non-fat yogurt

1 egg white

1/2 teaspoon cinnamon

1/2 teaspoon vanilla

6 CREPES (p. 201)

- Mix ingredients together and spoon into crepes.
- Fold ends and then sides of crepes.
- Place in lightly greased non-stick skillet, cover and cook for about 15 minutes over medium heat.
- Turn and cook another 5 minutes until browned.

Yield: 6 blintzes. One serving: 1 blintz.

Per serving:

calories	63
protein	6.6 grams
fat	0.7 grams
carbohydrate	7.8 grams
fiber	1.0 grams
cholesterol	16 milligrams
sodium	39 milligrams

Diabetes exchanges:

1/2 starch; 1/2 skim milk

CHEESE-BLUEBERRY BLINTZES

3 ounces unsalted hoop cheese

1/4 cup plain non-fat yogurt

1 egg white

1/2 teaspoon cinnamon

1/4 cup blueberries (fresh or frozen)

6 CREPES (p. 201)

- Mix ingredients together, addiing the blueberries last.
- Place a heaping tablespoon of mixture on each
crepe.
- Fold ends of crepe and then sides.
- Place in lightly greased non-stick skillet, cover,
and cook for about 15 minutes over medium
heat.
- Turn, and cook another 5 minutes, or until
blintzes are browned.

Yield: 6 blueberry-cheese blintzes.
One serving: 1 blintz

Per serving:

calories 61
protein . . . . 5.9 grams
fat . . . . 0.7 grams
carbohydrate . . . . 8.5 grams
fiber . . . . 1.2 grams
cholesterol . . . . 15 milligrams
sodium . . . . 39 milligrams

Diabetes exchanges

1/2 starch
1/2 skim milk

SERVING SUGGESTION:

Excellent as a main course served with plain non-fat yogurt.

SPINACH-MUSHROOM BLINTZES

1/2 cup chopped spinach (kale, beet greens or broccoli may be substituted)

1/4 cup lightly steamed mushrooms, chopped

1/4 cup lightly steamed onions, chopped

1/2 teaspoon SALT FREE SEASONING (p. 51), or 1/4 teaspoon each of oregano and basil

1/2 teaspooon lemon juice

6 CREPES (p. 201)

- Combine ingredients.
- Place a heaping tablespoon in each crepe.
- Fold ends and sides and place on lightly greasd, non-stick skillet.
- Cover and cook for 15 minutes over medium heat.
- Turn and cook another 10 minutes, or until browned.

Yield: 6 spinach-mushroom blintzes.
One serving: 1 crepe.

Per serving:

calories 46
protein . . . . 3.1 grams
fat . . . . 0.6 grams
carbohydrate . . . . 7.9 grams
fiber . . . . 1.5 grams
cholesterol . . . . 14 milligrams
sodium . . . . 32 milligrams

Diabetes exchanges:

1/2 starch
1/2 vegetable

FOR VARIETY—MAKE THE FOLLOWING:

BEAN BLINTZES with cooked BEANS (p. 114).

BROCCOLI-ONION BLINTZES with cooked and chopped broccoli and onions.

BUCKWHEAT GROATS-ONION BLINTZES with BUCKWHEAT GROATS (p. 121) and steamed onions.

POTATO BLINTZES with cooked and mashed potatoes.

RICE BLINTZES with cooked BROWN RICE (p. 152).

STRAWBERRY BLINTZES

1 cup sliced strawberries (fresh or frozen)
1 tablespoon unfiltered apple juice
1/2 teaspoon lemon juice
6 CREPES (p. 201)

- Mix strawberries and apple and lemon juices.
- Place 1/6 of mixture in each crepe.
- Fold ends and sides.
- Cook for 15 minutes in covered, lightly greased non-stick skillet.
- Turn, cover, and cook another 5 minutes, or until blintzes are browned.

Yield: 6 blintzes. One serving: 1 blintz

Per serving:

calories	48
protein	2.7 grams
fat	0.6 grams
carbohydrate	8.5 grams
fiber	1.6 grams
cholesterol	14 milligrams
sodium	21 milligrams

Diabetes exchanges:

1/2 starch

CEREALS

GRANOLA

4 cups rolled oats (not ready to eat cereal)
1 cup oat bran
1/2 cup rolled rye (not ready to eat cereal)
1/2 cup rolled barley (not ready to eat cereal)
1 tablespoon cinnamon
1/4 cup sesame seeds (optional)
1 cup unfiltered apple juice
1 tablespoon vanilla
6 cut up dates, mixed with 2 tablespoons whole wheat flour (optional)

- Combine all dry ingredients.
- Stir vanilla into apple juice and mix with dry ingredients.
- Mix in dates with flour.
- Spread mixture on two cookie sheets.
- Bake in oven preheated to 275 for 1/2 hour.
- Crumble granola and reduce heat to 225 degrees and cook until all of the mixture is dry (about 1 hour longer).
- Place in air tight containers until ready for use.

Yield: about 6 cups granola. One portion: 1/3 cup.

Per serving:

calories 108
protein . . . . 4.3 grams
fat . . . . 1.6 grams
carbohydrate . . . . 21.0 grams
fiber . . . . 3.7 grams
cholesterol . . . . 0 milligrams
sodium . . . . 1 milligram

Diabetes exchanges:

1 starch

FOR VARIETY:

Substitute rolled wheat and rolled triticale for part of the rye and barley.

HOT OATMEAL WITH BANANA

1/6 cup rolled oats (not ready to eat cereal)
1/6 cup oat bran
1/2 small banana, sliced (2 ounces)
1 cup water

- Place all ingredients in small pot and stir.
- Bring to a boil, reduce heat and simmer for 2-3 minutes with lid of pot tilted.

Yield: 1 portion (1 cup).

Per serving:

calories	142
protein	5.4 grams
fat	2.2 grams
carbohydrate	32.6 grams
fiber	4.8 grams
cholesterol	0 milligrams
sodium	2 milligrams

Diabetes exchanges:

1 starch
1 fruit

FOR VARIETY:

Instead of banana use 1 ounce raisins and 1/4 teaspoon cinnamon.

PANCAKES

POTATO PANCAKES (LATKES)

2 cups grated baking potatoes

1/3 cup chopped onions

2 egg whites, lightly beaten

1/8 teaspoon salt (optional, add 48 milligrams sodium per serving)

- Mix potatoes, onions, and salt (if used).
- Add egg whites and mix lightly.
- Lightly grease a non-stick skillet or stove top griddle and set heat on medium high.
- When a drop of water sizzles, the surface is hot enough.
- Place heaping tablespoons on the skillet and cook until one side is browned.
- Turn and cook until the second side is browned.
- If the pancakes are cooking too quickly so that the inside is not cooked enough for you, lower the heat and it will take longer for the outside to become brown. The inside will be cooked more thorougly.

Yield: 12 pancakes about 3 inches in diameter.
One serving: 2 pancakes.

Per serving:

calories	54
protein	2.1 grams
fat	0.1 grams
carbohydrate	11.3 grams
fiber	0.9 grams
cholesterol	0 milligrams
sodium	20 milligrams

Diabetes exchanges:

1 starch

SERVING SUGGESTION:

Serve with APPLESAUCE (p. 60).

FOR VARIETY—ZUCCHINI-POTATO PANCAKES:

Use 1/2 cup grated zucchini and 1-1/2 cups grated potatoes.

WHOLE WHEAT PANCAKES

1 cup whole wheat flour (preferably stone ground)

1 teaspoon baking powder (non-aluminum)

1 cup non-fat milk

1 teaspoon canola oil

pinch of salt (optional, less than 1/8 teaspoon, add 24 milligrams sodium per serving)

2 egg whites, beaten lightly

1 teaspoon sesame seeds

- Combine dry ingredients.
- Add milk, canola oil and egg whites.
- Cook on lightly greased griddle set at medium high heat. Griddle should sizzle when drops of water are sprinkled on it.

Yield: about 12 pancakes, 4 inches in diameter. One serving: 2 pancakes.

Per serving:

calories	98
protein	5.3 grams
fat	1.5 grams
carbohydrate	16.7 grams
fiber	2.5 grams
cholesterol	1 milligram
sodium	90

1-1/2 starch

BLUEBERRY PANCAKES

Use the recipe for WHOLE WHEAT PANCAKES, but add 1 cup frozen blueberries mixed with 2 tablespoons of whole wheat flour.

WHOLE WHEAT WAFFLES

Use the recipe for WHOLE WHEAT PANCAKES, but place mixture in a waffle iron. Add 1 cup of frozen blueberries for BLUEBERRY WAFFLES.

FOR VARIETY—BUCKWHEAT PANCAKES or WAFFLES:

Use 3/4 cup buckwheat flour and 1/4 cup whole wheat flour.

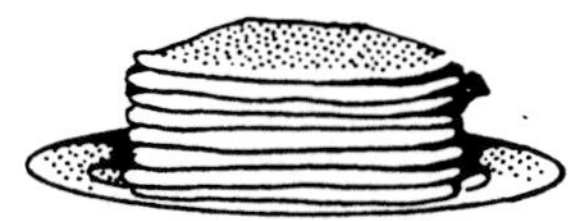

CHAPTER 8

DESSERTS

APPLE CRISP

10 medium apples, peeled and cored, each cut into 8 pieces (should measure about 6 cups)

1/2 cup unfiltered apple juice

1 teaspoon vanilla

1/4 cup lemon juice

1 tablespoon cinnamon

1 scant tablespoon raisins

- Place apple pieces in pot and sprinkle with lemon juice.
- Stir vanilla in apple juice and add to apples.
- Mix in cinnamon and raisins.
- Cook over medium heat until apples are done, but be careful not to overcook or the apples will fall apart.

CRUST

1-1/4 cups rolled oats (not ready-to-eat cereal)

1/4 cup oat bran

1 teaspoon cinnamon

1/2 cup unfiltered apple juice or 1/2 cup orange juice

1 teaspoon vanilla

2 teaspoons canola oil

- Mix dry ingredients.
- Mix vanilla in apple juice and add to dry in-
  gredients.
- Mix in canola oil and place 1/4 cup mixture on
  non-stick pan. (For top of apple crisp)
- Press the rest of mixture onto lightly greased
  pie dish.
- Place both pans into oven preheated to 325
  degrees.
- Bake 1/4 cup mixture for 15 minutes, or until
  flakes are browned and crisp.
- Bake pie shell for 25 minutes, or until crust is
  crisp. Makes 1 crust.
- Pour apple mixture into pie crust.
- Sprinkle top with separate toasted oat mixture
  and refrigerate until ready to eat.

Yield: 12 pieces. One serving: 1/12 of apple crisp.

Per serving:

calories	122
protein	1.9 grams
fat	1.8 grams
carbohydrate	27.0 grams
fiber	4.3 grams
cholesterol	0 milligrams
sodium	1 milligram

Diabetes exchanges:

1 starch; 1 fruit

APPLESAUCE CAKE

2 cups whole wheat flour (preferably stone ground)

1/2 cup oat bran

2 teaspoons baking powder (non-aluminum)

3/4 teaspoon cinnamon

3/4 teaspoon allspice

3/4 teaspoon cloves

1 tablespoon vanilla

1 cup unfiltered apple juice

1-1/2 cup thick, unsweetened APPLESAUCE (p. 60)

2 teaspoons canola oil

2 egg whites, beaten but not stiff

- Combine dry ingredients.
- Mix vanilla with apple juice and add to dry ingredients.
- Add applesauce, canola oil and egg whites.
- Place in lightly greased loaf pan (about 8 by 5 by 2-1/2 inches) and bake in oven preheated to 350 for 50 minutes or until knife inserted in the center comes out clean.

Yield: 16 pieces 1/2 inch thick.
One serving: 1 slice.

Per serving:

calories 86
protein . . . . 3.0 grams
fat . . . . 1.1 grams
carbohydrate . . . . 17.8 grams
fiber . . . . 2.8 grams
cholesterol . . . . 0 milligrams
sodium . . . . 46 milligrams

Diabetes exchanges:

1 starch

SERVING SUGGESTION:

May be used as a healthful birthday cake. CARROT CAKE (p. 231) is also excellent for birthdays.

APRICOT PIE

2 cups stewed apricots

1/4 cup apricot juice

2 tablespoons lemon juice

1/4 teaspoon cloves

3 egg whites, beaten moderately

1 pie crust (see CRUST in APPLE CRISP, p. 223)

- Mix apricots, apricot juice, lemon juice and cloves together.
- Fold in egg whites.
- Pour into unbaked pie shell and bake in oven preheated to 350 degrees for 25 minutes.
- Chill before serving.

Yield: 12 portions. One serving: I/12 of pie.

Per serving:

calories	69
protein	2.9 grams
fat	1.5 grams
carbohydrate	12.1grams
fiber	1.4 grams
cholesterol	0 milligrams
sodium	15 milligrams

1 starch

> # FOR VARIETY:
>
> *Substitute peaches (PEACH PIE),*
> *nectarines (NECTARINE PIE)*
> *or berries (BERRY PIE) for apricots.*

CAROB OATMEAL COOKIES

1/2 cup rolled oats (not ready to eat cereal)

1/3 cup oat bran

1/4 cup whole wheat flour (preferably stone ground)

1/3 cup carob powder

1/8 teaspoon baking powder

1 teaspoon cinnamon

2 scant tablespoons chopped unsalted walnuts

1/4 cup undiluted frozen apple juice, thawed

1/4 cup plus 2 tablespoons unfiltered apple juice

1 teaspoon vanilla

1 teaspoon canola oil

* Combine dry ingredients including nuts.
* Combine apple juices, vanilla and canola oil and mix with dry ingredients.
* Drop on lightly greased cookie sheet and bake in oven preheated to 375 degrees for about 10 minutes.

Yield: 16 cookies, 2 inches in diameter.
One serving: 2 cookies.

Per serving:

calories 96
protein . . . . 2.4 grams
fat . . . . 2.4 grams
carbohydrate . . . . 18.2 grams
fiber . . . . 3.2 grams
cholesterol . . . . 0 milligrams
sodium . . . . 8 milligrams

Diabetes exchanges:

1 starch

FOR VARIETY:

If you prefer, these cookies may be made without nuts.

May be frozen to be used as needed.

CARROT CAKE

2 cups whole wheat pastry flour (preferably stone ground)

2 teaspoons baking powder

2 teaspoons cinnamon

1/2 teaspoon ginger

1-3/4 cups unfiltered apple juice

1/4 cup pineapple juice (from crushed pineapple can)

2 teaspoons vanilla

2 cups finely grated carrots

1/4 cup crushed pineapple (no added sugar)

2 teaspoons canola oil

2 egg whites, beaten but not stiff

1/8 cup raisins

- Mix flour with baking powder, cinnamon and ginger.
- Stir apple juice, pineapple juice and vanilla together and add to flour mixture.
- Add carrots, pineapple, canola oil and raisins and mix thoroughly.
- Fold in egg whites.

- Place mixture into lightly greased baking pan (about 7 by 15 inches) and place in oven preheated to 350 degrees.
- Bake for 1 hour, or until knife inserted in the center comes out dry.

Yield: 14 pieces. One serving: 1 piece.

Per serving:

calories	99
protein	3.1 grams
fat	0.7 grams
carbohydrate	18.5 grams
fiber	2.9 grams
cholesterol	0 milligrams
sodium	58 milligrams

Diabetes exchanges:

1 starch

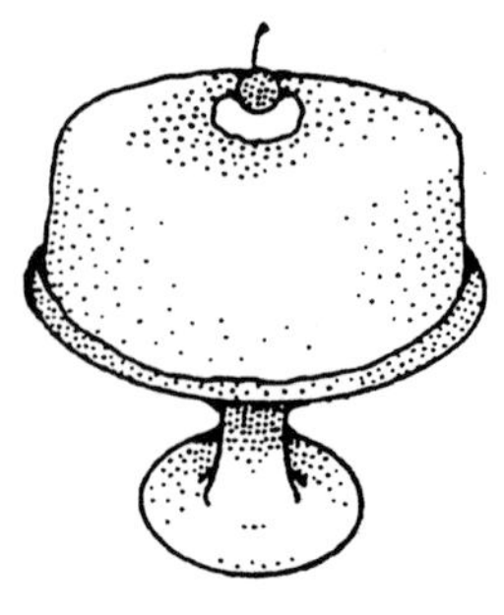

OATMEAL RAISIN COOKIES

1/2 cup rolled oats (not ready to eat cereal)

1/3 cup oat bran

1/4 cup whole wheat flour (preferably stone ground)

1/8 teaspoon baking powder

1/2 teaspoon allspice

1/4 cup undiluted frozen apple juice, thawed

1/4 cup unfiltered apple juice

1/2 teaspoon vanilla

1 teaspoon canola oil

1/2 ounce raisins

- Combine dry ingredients.
- Combine apple juices, vanilla, canola oil and raisins and mix with dry ingredients.
- Drop on lightly greased cookie sheet.
- Bake in oven preheated to 350 degrees for about 10 minutes.

Yield: 12 cookies 2 inches in diameter.
One serving: 2 cookies.

Per serving:

calories	96
protein	2.8 grams
fat	1.8 grams
carbohydrate	19.8 grams
fiber	2.4 grams
cholesterol	0 milligrams
sodium	11 milligrams

Diabetes exchanges:

1 starch

FOR VARIETY:

Substitute pieces of dates or dried apricots for the raisins.

PRUNE-APPLE WHIP

1/2 cup cooked prunes, puréed
1/2 cup APPLESAUCE (p. 60)
1/4 teaspoon nutmeg
1/4 teaspoon cloves
1/4 teaspoon cinnamon
2 egg whites, beaten lightly

- Combine prunes, applesauce, nutmeg, cloves and cinnamon.
- Add egg whites.
- Pour into small lightly greased baking dish.
- Bake in oven preheated to 350 degrees for about 50 minutes, or until knife inserted in the center comes out dry.
- Serve warm or cold.

Yield: 1 cup. One serving: 1/2 cup.

Per serving:

calories 88
protein . . . . 4.2 grams
fat . . . . 0.4 grams
carbohydrate . . . . 32.6 grams
fiber . . . . 3.2 grams
cholesterol . . . . 0 milligrams
sodium . . . . 54 milligrams

Diabetes exchanges:

1 fruit

FOR VARIETY:

Substitute cooked apricots, peaches or nectarines for prunes.

RICE PUDDING

1/2 cup brown rice

1-1/2 cups non-fat milk

1/3 cup water

1/8 teaspoon salt (optional, add 72 milligrams sodium per serving)

2 egg whites, beaten but not stiff

1/2 ounce raisins

1 teaspoon vanilla

1/2 teaspoon cinnamon

- Place rice, milk, water and salt (if used) in medium saucepan and bring to a boil.
- Reduce heat and simmer covered for 25 minutes.
- Pour mixture into casserole.
- In a separate bowl combine egg whites, raisins, vanilla and cinnamon.
- Add to casserole and mix ingredients.
- Place in oven preheated to 325 degrees and bake for 20 minutes, or until a knife inserted in the center comes out dry.
- Serve warm or chilled.

Yield: 2 cups pudding. One portion: 1/2 cup.

Per serving:

calories 141
protein . . . . 6.8 grams
fat . . . . 0.9 grams
carbohydrate . . . . 25.9 grams
fiber . . . . 1.1 grams
cholesterol . . . . 2 milligrams
sodium . . . . 76 milligrams

Diabetes exchanges:

1 starch
1/2 lean meat/fish
1/2 fruit

SERVING SUGGESTION:

A good dessert with a meal containing beans or lentils.

YAM PIE

2 cups baked yams (about 3 medium yams)

4 egg whites, beaten moderately

1 can skimmed non-fat milk, 12 ounces

1 teaspoon cinnamon

1/2 teaspoon nutmeg

1/2 teaspoon ginger

1/2 teaspoon cloves

1 uncooked pie crust without top pieces (see CRUST in APPLE CRISP, p. 223)

- Mix ingredients together.
- Pour into unbaked pie shell and bake for 15 minutes in oven preheated to 450 degrees.
- Reduce heat to 350 degrees and bake an additional 45 minutes, or until knife inserted in center comes out dry.
- Chill before serving.

Yield: one pie, 12 pieces. One serving: 1 piece.

Per serving:

calories 105
protein . . . . 5.3 grams
fat . . . . 1.6 grams
carbohydrate . . . . 18.3 grams
fiber . . . . 1.3 grams
cholesterol . . . . 1 milligram
sodium . . . . 53 milligrams

Diabetes exchanges:

1 starch

FOR VARIETY:

Use sweet potatoes (SWEET POTATO PIE) instead of yams.

FRUITS AND FRUIT JUICES

APRICOT, PRUNE, BANANA NUT, WHOLE WHEAT BLUEBERRY, and DATE-BRAN MUFFINS and APPLE and STRAWBERRY BLINTZES are excellent desserts.

FRESH FRUITS are very wholesome desserts. Fruits contain more fiber than fruit juices. Some examples of diabetes exchanges for fruits are included here. Each item on the list equals 1 exchange.*

Fresh Fruit

Apple	1/2 medium apple (4 inches in diameter)
Apricots	4 medium, fresh
Banana	1/2 banana (9 inches long)
Blackberries . . .	3/4 cup
Blueberries . . .	3/4 cup
Cantaloupe . . .	1 cup of cubes
Cherries	12 raw
Figs	2 (fresh, 2 inches in diameter)
Grapefruit	1/2 medium
Grapes	15 small
Honeydew melon	1 cup of cubes
Kiwi	1 large
Mango	1/2 small

Nectarine . . . . . 1 nectarine (1-1/2 inches
in diameter)
Orange . . . . 1 orange (2-1/2 inches
in diameter)
Papaya . . . . 1 cup of cubes
Peach . . . . 1 (2-3/4 inches in diameter)
Pear . . . . 1/2 large
Pineapple . . . . . 3/4 cup
Plum . . . . 2 (2 inches in diameter)
Raspberries . . . 1 cup fresh
Strawberries . . . 1-1/4 cup whole fresh
Tangerines . . . . 2 (2-1/2 inches in diameter)
Watermelon . . . 1-1/4 cups of cubes

Dried Fruit:

Apples . . . . 4 rings
Apricots . . . . . 7 halves
Dates . . . . 2-1/2 medium
Figs . . . . 1-1/2 medium
Prunes . . . . . . 3 medium
Raisins . . . . . . 2 tablespoons

Fruit Juices:

Apple juice . . . . 1/2 cup
Cranberry juice . 1/3 cup
Grapefruit juice . 1/2 cup
Grape juice . . . . 1/3 cup
Orange juice . . . 1/2 cup
Pineapple juice . . 1/2 cup
Prune juice . . . . 1/3 cup

*Source: American Diabetes Association, Inc. and The American Dietetic Association, *Exchange Lists for Meal Planning* (available in large print).

APPENDIX

MENUS

BREAKFAST SUGGESTIONS

Hot oatmeal with banana (p. 214)

1/2 cup non-fat milk

1/2 grapefruit

Whole wheat pancakes (p. 218)

1/2 cup applesauce (p. 60)

1 sliced orange

---

1 oat bran muffin (p. 177)

1 sliced orange

Blueberry waffles (p. 219)

1/2 cup non-fat plain yogurt

1/2 grapefruit

Granola (p. 212)

1/2 cup non-fat milk

1 sliced orange

<u>**MID-MORNING SNACK**</u>

1 medium apple or another fresh fruit

1 piece whole grain toast

<u>**LUNCH**</u>

Any salad (pages 23 through 47)

1 blueberry muffin (p. 171)

1 sliced orange or other citrus fruit

Chicken tostada (p. 86)

1 apple

1 pumpkin muffin (p. 179)

Cheese blintzes (p. 205)

1/2 cup applesauce (p. 60)

1/2 cup non-fat plain yogurt

1/2 ear steamed corn on the cob

Stuffed chapati (p. 126)

Kiwi or tangerine

Tuna-egg white sandwich (p. 45)

Apple

AFTERNOON SNACK

1 muffin (p. 166 through p. 180)

1 apple

Carrot sticks

DINNER

Bean soup (p. 3)

Mixed salad (p. 43)

Broccoli rice bake (p. 117)

1/2 cup steamed carrots

Plum sauce (p. 64)

Whole wheat French roll (p. 195)

Orange slices

Vegetable soup with barley (p. 21)

Chicken stir fry (p. 83)

Brown rice (p. 152)

1/2 grapefruit

Whole wheat roll or bread (p. 187-190)

Beet soup (p. 5)

1/4 cup non-fat yogurt (place in soup)

1 boiled potato (place in soup)

Broccoli and onion blintzes (p. 209)

Orange slices
Banana bread (p. 182)

Cabbage soup (p. 9)
Turkey loaf (p. 106)
Cranberry apple sauce (p. 62)
Asparagus with shallots (p. 111)
Carrot sticks
Yam pie (p. 239)

Azuki beans with pasta (p. 112)
Brussels sprouts casserole (p. 119)
Pear sauce (p. 61)
Carrot cake (p. 231)

HOLIDAY DINNER

Potato pancakes (p. 216)
Applesauce (p. 60)
Roast turkey (skin and fat removed)
Cranberry apple sauce (p. 62)
Yams and apples (p. 161)
Zucchini with water chestnuts (p. 163)
Whole wheat rolls (p. 190)
Apple crisp (p. 223)

<u>**BEDTIME SNACK**</u>

Whole grain toast
1/2 banana

<u>**HORS D'OEUVRES**</u>

- **Mini cheese blintzes (p. 205) with applesauce (p. 60) and non-fat yogurt**
- **Mini muffins (p. 166 through p. 180) baked in muffin pan with 1 to 1-1/2 sections (they will take less time to bake than regular muffins)**
- **Mini potato pancakes (p. 216)**
- **Small pieces of poached salmon (p. 95) with a dash of mustard served on Belgian endive**
- **Tabouli (p. 153) with crackers**
- **2 inch turkey burgers (p. 106) on small pieces of toast**
- **Turkey cocktail nuggets (p. 103) or beef cocktail nuggets (p. 105)**
- **Cut up vegetables with yogurt-hoop cheese dip (p. 57)**

Note: People with diabetes may require adjustments of foods according to their insulin or oral medication prescriptions and exercise and activity regimen. It is best to avoid eating large

amounts of carbohydrates at one time. Discuss your particular needs with your doctor or dietitian.

TABLE 1

SATURATED FAT AND CHOLESTEROL CONTENT OF SELECTED FOODS

FOOD	QUANTITY	SATURATED FAT (grams)	CHOLESTEROL (milligrams)
Beef	3-1/2 ounces	6.2	87.5
Brains	3 ounces	NA	>1700
Butter	1 tablespoon	8.7	36
Buttermilk	1 cup	1.3	9
Cheese, American	1 ounce	5.7	27
Cheese, cheddar	1 ounce	6.0	30
Chicken, turkey,			
dark meat, no skin	3-1/2 ounces	2.7	93
light meat, no skin	3-1/2 ounces	1.3	95.1
Cottage cheese, creamed	1/2 cup	3.2	24

FOOD	QUANTITY	SATURATED FAT (grams)	CHOLESTEROL (milligrams)
Egg	1 large egg or 1 yolk	1.7	274
Egg noodles	1 cup	0.5	50
Frankfurter, all meat	1	5.4	22
Halibut, cooked	3 ounces	0.4	35
Ice cream, regular	1/2 cup	7.4	27
Ice milk	1/2 cup	1.7	13
Kidney	3-1/2 ounces	NA	793
Lamb	3-1/2 ounces	8.8	99
Liver	3-1/2 ounces	NA	443
Mackerel, cooked	3-1/2 ounces	2.0	49
Mayonnaise	1 tablespoon	1.7	6
Milk, non-fat	1 cup	0.3	4
Milk, whole	1 cup	4.9	34
Salmon, cooked	3-1/2 ounces	1.8	47
Sardines, canned in oil	3 ounces	1.6	128

FOOD	QUANTITY	SATURATED FAT (grams)	CHOLESTEROL (milligrams)
Tuna, canned in water	3-1/2 ounces	0.7	41
Yogurt, low fat	1 cup	2.3	17

- Cereals and grains, vegetables, legumes and fruits have no cholesterol and trace amounts of saturated fat.

- NA: Information not available.

- Several items are not recommended for a low fat, low cholesterol, low sodium and high complex carbohydrate, high fiber diet but are included for purposes of comparison.

Sources: Select Committee on Nutrition and Human Needs, United States Senate, "Dietary Goals for the United States," 1977.

Jean A.T. Pennington, Ph.D., R.D., and Helen Nichols Church, B.S. *Bowes and Church's Food Values of Portions Commonly Used,* 1985.

TABLE 2

ANALYSIS OF FATTY ACID CONTENT OF FATS AND OILS

TYPE OF FAT (1 tablespoon)	CHOLES-TEROL (milligrams)	SATURATED (grams)	MONOUNSAT-URATED (grams)	POLYUNSAT-URATED (grams)
Beef fat	14	11.7	6.1	5.2
Butter	31	7.1	3.3	0.4
Canola oil	0	1.0	9.0	4.0
Chicken fat	11	3.8	6.3	2.7
Coconut oil	0	12.1	0.8	0.3
Corn oil	0	1.7	3.3	7.8
Mayonnaise	8	2.0	2.4	5.6
Olive oil	0	1.9	9.7	1.1
Palm oil	0	7.2	5.0	1.4
Peanut oil	0	2.3	6.2	4.2
Safflower oil	0	1.3	1.6	10.0

TYPE OF FAT (1 tablespoon)	CHOLES-TEROL (milligrams)	SATURATED (grams)	MONOUNSAT-URATED (grams)	POLYUNSAT-URATED (grams)
Sesame oil	0	2.1	5.5	5.7
Soybean oil	0	2.1	3.2	8.1
Sunflower oil	0	1.5	2.9	8.9

- It is advisable to consume very little fat. Choose fats with a low cholesterol and saturated fatty acid content. There are oils listed here which are not recommended (coconut and palm oil). It is best to avoid beef fat, butter, chicken fat and other fats which solidify at room temperature.

Sources: Jane Brody, *Jane Brody's Nutrition Book*, 1982, from the American Heart Association.

Jean A.T. Pennington, Ph.D., R.D., and Helen Nichols Church, B.S. *Bowes and Church's Food Values of Portions Commonly Used*, 1985.

Loriva Supreme Foods, Inc. (canola oil).

TABLE 3

SODIUM AND POTASSIUM CONTENT OF SELECTED FOODS

FOOD	QUANTITY	SODIUM (milligrams)	POTASSIUM (milligrams)
Bread, whole wheat	1 slice	132	68
Cheese, American	1 ounce	341	25
Cheese, cottage	3-1/2 ounces	228	104
Corn Flakes, Kellogg's	1 ounce	282	15
Egg	1	61	65
Frankfurter	1	555	110
Milk, whole	1/2 cup	120	346
Oatmeal, cooked	3-1/2 ounces	2	61
Olives, black	2 large	150	5
Pickle, dill	1 medium	928	130
Potato, baking	3-1/2 ounces	4	323

FOOD	QUANTITY	SODIUM (milligrams)	POTASSIUM (milligrams)
Salmon, canned	3-1/2 ounces	522	349
Salmon, canned, salt free	3-1/2 ounces	48	391
Salt	1 teaspoon	2300	0
Sauerkraut	1 cup	1755	296
Tuna, canned	3-1/2 ounces	899	240
Tuna, canned, salt free	3-1/2 ounces	46	382

- Vegetables, fresh without added salt, very low in sodium (0 to 20 milligrams per 3-1/2 ounces): broccoli, cabbage, cauliflower, corn, eggplant, legumes, onions, potatoes, radishes, tomatoes, sweet potatoes.
- Vegetables, fresh without added salt, moderate amounts of sodium (23-69 milligrams per 3-1/2 ounces): beets, carrots, kale, parsley, spinach, turnips and watercress.
- Vegetables, fresh without added salt, larger amounts of sodium (75 to 126 milligrams per 3-1/2 ounces): beet greens, celery and Swiss chard.

- Some of these foods are not recommended for a low cholesterol, low fat and low sodium diet but are included here for analysis.

<u>Sources</u>: Select Committee on Nutrition and Human Needs, United States Senate, "Dietary Goals for the United States," 1977.

Jean A.T. Pennington, Ph.D., R.D., and Helen Nichols Church, B.S. *Bowes and Church's Food Values of Portions Commonly Used.* 1985.

TABLE 4

FIBER CONTENT OF SELECTED FOODS

FOOD	QUANTITY	CALORIES	FIBER (grams)
Apple	1/2 large	42	2.0
Apricots, fresh	2	32	1.4
Asparagus, cooked	1/2 cup	18	3.5
Banana, fresh	1/2 medium	48	1.5
Bean sprouts	1/2 cup	13	1.5
Beans, green, cooked	1/2 cup	10	2.1
Beans, kidney, cooked	1/2 cup	94	9.7
Beans, lima, cooked	1/2 cup	63	8.3
Beans, pinto, cooked	1/2 cup	78	8.9
Beans, white, cooked	1/2 cup	79	7.9
Beets, cooked	1/2 cup	33	2.1
Blackberries	3/4 cup	40	6.7

FOOD	QUANTITY	CALORIES	FIBER (grams)
Bread			
pumpernickel	3/4 slice	58	1.4
French	1 slice	71	0.7
rye	1 slice	62	0.8
wheat	1 slice	59	1.3
Broccoli, cooked	1/2 cup	18	3.5
Brussels sprouts, cooked	1/2 cup	20	2.3
Cabbage, white, cooked	1/2 cup	10	2.1
Carrots, raw	1/2 cup	15	1.8
Cauliflower, cooked	1/2 cup	14	1.6
Celery, raw	1/2 cup	8	1.1
Cereal			
All Bran	1/3 cup	70	8.4
Corn Chex	3/4 cup	71	2.6
Corn Flakes	3/4 cup	70	2.6
Nutri-Grain, wheat	1/2 cup	67	1.2
Grape Nuts	3 tablespoons	70	2.7

FOOD	QUANTITY	CALORIES	FIBER (grams)
Oat Bran, dry	1/4 cup	58	5.3
Oatmeal, dry	1/4 cup	71	2.9
Puffed Wheat	3/4 cup	68	3.4
Shredded Wheat	1 biscuit	70	2.8
Total	3/4 cup	75	2.5
Wheaties	3/4 cup	73	2.6
Cherries, fresh	10 large	38	1.1
Corn, fresh	1/2 medium ear	72	2.6
Crackers			
graham	2 squares	53	1.4
rye	3	64	2.3
saltines	6	76	0.8
Cranberries	1/2 cup	31	4.0
Cucumber	1/2 cup	5	1.1
Eggplant, raw	1/2 cup	16	2.5
Fig, dried	1 medium	46	3.7
Grapefruit	1/2 medium	31	0.8

FOOD	QUANTITY	CALORIES	FIBER (grams)
Grapes, black	15	45	0.5
Grapes, white	10	36	0.5
Kale, cooked	1/2 cup	15	1.3
Lentils, cooked	1/2 cup	97	3.7
Lettuce	1 cup	5	0.8
Melon			
cantaloupe	1 cup	39	1.6
honeydew	1 cup	42	1.5
watermelon	1 cup	35	1.4
Mushrooms	1/2 cup	7	0.9
Mustard greens, raw	1 cup	7	0.2
Nectarine, raw	1 small	44	1.5
Nuts			
almonds	1 tablespoon	46	1.1
chestnuts	3	46	1.8
peanuts	1 tablespoon	52	0.8
pecans	1 tablespoon	49	0.5
walnuts	1 tablespoon	49	0.2

FOOD	QUANTITY	CALORIES	FIBER (grams)
Okra, raw	1/2 cup	13	1.6
Onion, raw	1/2 cup	14	1.2
Orange	small	35	1.6
Peach, fresh	1 medium	38	2.3
Pear	1/2 medium	44	2.0
Peas, cooked	1/2 cup	60	3.8
Pepper, green, raw	1/2 cup	10	1.1
Pineapple, raw	1/2 cup	41	0.8
Plums	3 small	38	1.8
Popcorn, popped	3 cups	62	3.0
Potato, baked sweet	1/2 medium	79	2.1
Potato, baked white	1/2 medium	72	1.0
Prunes, dried	2 medium	38	2.8
Radishes, raw	1/2 cup	7	1.3
Raisins	1-1/2 tablespoons	39	1.0
Raspberries	1 cup	42	9.2
Rice, brown	1/3 cup	72	1.6
Rice, white	1/3 cup	76	0.5

FOOD	QUANTITY	CALORIES	FIBER (grams)
Spaghetti	1/2 cup	76	0.8
Spinach, raw	1 cup	8	0.2
Squash			
summer, cooked	1/2 cup	8	2.0
winter, cooked	1/2 cup	82	7.0
Strawberries	1 cup	45	3.1
Tangerine	1 large	39	2.0
Tomato, cooked	1/2 cup	20	1.5
Tomato, raw	1 small	18	1.5
Yam, cooked	1/3 cup	72	2.6
Zucchini, raw	1/2 cup	7	2.0

Sources: James W. Anderson, M.D., *Diabetes: A Practical Guide to Healthy Living.* HCF Diabetes Foundation, Inc., P.O. Box 22124, Lexington, KY 40522.

Jean A.T. Pennington, Ph.D., R.D. and Helen Nichols Church, B.S., *Bowes & Church's Food Values of Portions Commonly Used,* 1985.

TABLE 5

PROTEIN CONTENT OF SELECTED FOODS

FOOD	QUANTITY	PROTEIN (grams)
<u>FOODS HIGH IN PROTEIN</u>		
Beef, ground, broiled	3-1/2 ounces	26.0
Cheese		
American	1 ounce	6.3
brick	1 ounce	6.6
cheddar	1 ounce	7.1
cottage, low fat	1/4 cup	7.0
cottage, dry curd	1/4 cup	6.2
jack	1 ounce	6.9
mozzarella	1 ounce	5.5
parmesan, grated	1 tablespoon	2.1
ricotta, part skim	1/4 cup	7.0

FOOD	QUANTITY	PROTEIN (grams)
Swiss	1 ounce	8.1
Swiss, processed	1 ounce	7.0
Egg, whole	1 large, boiled	6.1
Egg, white	1 large	3.4
Fish		
bass, striped	3-1/2 ounces	18.9
cod	3-1/2 ounces	17.6
halibut	3-1/2 ounces	19.8
perch	3-1/2 ounces	19.5
red snapper	3-1/2 ounces	19.8
salmon	3-1/2 ounces	22.5
sardines, tomato sauce	1 can	18
sole	3-1/2 ounces	14.9
trout, lake	3-1/2 ounces	14.3
tuna, albacore	3-1/2 ounces	25.3
whitefish	3-1/2 ounces	18.9
Lamb, leg, roasted	3-1/2 ounces	20.6

FOOD	QUANTITY	PROTEIN (grams)
Milk and Yogurt		
buttermilk	1 cup	8.1
milk, whole	1 cup	8.0
milk, low fat (1%)	1 cup	8.0
milk, non-fat	1 cup	8.4
yogurt, low fat	1 cup	11.9
yogurt, non-fat	1 cup	13.0
Poultry		
chicken, light meat, no skin, broiled	3-1/2 ounces	30.9
chicken, dark meat, no skin, broiled	3-1/2 ounces	27.4
turkey, light meat, no skin, roasted	3-1/2 ounces	29.9
turkey, dark meat, no skin, roasted	3-1/2 ounces	28.6
veal, roasted	3-1/2 ounces	27.9

FOODS HIGH IN STARCH

Legumes

black-eyed peas	1/2 cup cooked	6.5

FOOD	QUANTITY	PROTEIN (grams)
garbanzo beans	1/2 cup cooked	10.2
kidney beans	1/2 cup cooked	5.6
lentils	1/2 cup cooked	5.6
lima beans	1/2 cup cooked	12.5
peas, split	1/2 cup cooked	7.3
soybeans	1/2 cup cooked	11.0
Bread		
cracked wheat	1 slice (1 ounce)	2.3
French	1 slice (1 ounce)	2.4
rye	1 slice (1 ounce)	2.1
tortilla, corn	1	2.1
whole wheat	1 slice (1 ounce)	2.4
Cereals, dry		
All Bran	1/3 cup	4.0
Bran Flakes, Kellogg's	3/4 cup	3.6
Cheerios	1-1/4 cup	4.3
Corn Flakes, Kellogg's	1-1/4 cup	2.3

FOOD	QUANTITY	PROTEIN (grams)
Grape Nuts	1/4 cup	3.3
Nutri-Grain, corn	2/3 cup	2.3
Nutri-Grain, wheat	3/4 cup	2.5
Puffed Rice	1 cup	0.9
Puffed Wheat	1 cup	2.2
Shredded Wheat	1 biscuit	2.6
Special K	1-1/3 cup	5.6
Total	1 cup	2.8
Wheaties	1 cup	2.7
Cereals, cooked		
Cream of Rice	3/4 cup	1.6
Cream of Wheat	3/4 cup	2.9
Oat Bran	3/4 cup (1/3 cup dry)	6.0
Oatmeal	3/4 cup (1/3 cup dry)	5.0
Ralston	3/4 cup	4.2
Roman Meal	3/4 cup	5.4
Wheatena	3/4 cup	3.7

FOOD	QUANTITY	PROTEIN (grams)
Crackers, snacks		
crispbread	1 thick or 2 thin slices	1.0
matzo	1 whole piece	3.0
melba toast	2 slices	1.0
popcorn	1 cup, dry	1.8
rice cakes	2 cakes	2.0
Ry Krisp	2 whole pieces	1.3
Grains:		
barley, dry	1 ounce	2.9
buckwheat groats, dry	1 ounce	3.0
corn	4 inches	3.3
rice, cooked	1/2 cup	2.3
Pasta (macaroni, noodles, spaghetti)	1/2 cup	3.7

FOODS LOW IN PROTEIN

Vegetables

asparagus	1/2 cup cooked	1.7

FOOD	QUANTITY	PROTEIN (grams)
beans, green	1/2 cup cooked	1.0
beets	1/2 cup cooked	0.9
broccoli	1/2 cup cooked	2.3
brussels sprouts	3-4, cooked	2.1
cabbage	1/2 cup cooked	1.0
carrots	1/2 cup cooked	0.5
cauliflower	1/2 cup cooked	1.1
chard	1/2 cup cooked	1.5
eggplant	1/2 cup cooked	1.0
kale	1/2 cup cooked	2.1
mushrooms	10 small, raw	2.7
potato, russet, baked	1 medium	2.6
potato, new (boiled)	1 medium	2.1
potato, sweet, baked	1 small	2.1
spinach	1/2 cup cooked	2.7
squash, summer	1/2 cup cooked	0.9
squash, winter	1/2 cup	1.8

FOOD	QUANTITY	PROTEIN (grams)
tomato	1 medium, raw	1.6
yam, baked	1 small	2.4
Fruits		
apple	1 medium	0.3
apricots	3 medium	1.5
banana	1/2 medium	0.6
blueberries	1 cup	1.0
cantaloupe	1 cup pieces	1.4
cherries	10 medium	0.8
cranberries	1 cup	0.4
dates	2	0.3
fig, raw	1 medium	0.4
grapefruit	1/2 medium	0.7
grapes	15 small white	0.6
nectarine	1 medium	1.3
orange	1 medium	1.4
peach	1 medium	0.6

FOOD	QUANTITY	PROTEIN (grams)
pear	1 medium	0.7
pineapple	1 cup pieces	0.6
plum	1 medium	0.5
prunes	2 medium	0.4
raisins	2 tablespoons	0.5
strawberries	1 cup	0.9
tangerine	1 medium	0.5
watermelon	1 cup pieces	1.0

FOODS HIGH IN FAT

FOOD	QUANTITY	PROTEIN (grams)
Avocado	1/8 medium	0.5
Nuts		
almonds	6 (1/4 ounce)	1.4
almond butter	1-1/2 teaspoons	1.5
cashews	4 (1/4 ounce)	1.7
peanuts	10 large (1/4 ounce)	1.9
peanut butter	1-1/2 teaspoons	1.9

FOOD	QUANTITY	PROTEIN (grams)
pecans	5 halves	0.6
pistachios	15 whole (1/4 ounce)	1.5
walnuts	5 halves (1/4 ounce)	1.3
Oil (canola, corn, cottonseed, olive, peanut, safflower, sesame, soybean)	1 teaspoon	0.0
Olives, black	8 medium	0.2
Olives, green	6 medium	0.2
Seeds		
pumpkin	1/4 ounce	2.0
sunflower	1/4 ounce	1.7
squash	1/4 ounce	2.0
soybean kernel	1/4 ounce	3.3

Source: Pennington, Jean A.T., Ph.D., R.D. and Church, Helen Nichols. *Bowes and Church's Food Values of Portions Commonly Used.* 1985.

TABLE 6

PHOSPHOROUS CONTENT OF SELECTED FOODS

FOOD	QUANTITY	PHOSPHOROUS (milligrams)
Beverages		
coffee, tea	1 cup	5
instant breakfast with milk	1 cup	390
Postum	1 cup	60
Bread products		
bread, white or rye	1 slice	25
bread, wheat	1 slice	55
graham crackers	2	20
pancakes	1 (4 inches)	65
rice, white	1/2 cup	20
rice, brown	1/2 cup	70
spaghetti	1/2 cup	40

FOOD	QUANTITY	PHOSPHOROUS (milligrams)
Cereals		
All Bran	1/2 cup	250
Cheerios	1/2 cup	55
Cream of Wheat or Rice	1/2 cup cooked	20
Grape Nuts	1/4 cup	20
Oatmeal	1/2 cup cooked	67
Puffed Wheat	1/2 cup	17
Rice Krispies	1/2 cup	15
Shredded Wheat	1/2 cup (1 biscuit)	100
Dairy products		
Cheese		
blue	1 ounce	110
cheddar	1 ounce	145
cottage	1/3 cup	100
cream	1 ounce	30
monterey jack	1 ounce	125
mozzarella	1 ounce	135

FOOD	QUANTITY	PHOSPHOROUS (milligrams)
parmesan	1 ounce	230
ricotta	1/3 cup	140
Swiss	1 ounce	175
Milk		
buttermilk	1 cup	220
evaporated	1 cup	520
milk shake	1 cup	285
whole	1 cup	290
non-fat	1 cup	250
Yogurt	1 cup	330

Fruit and fruit juices

Most fruits and fruit juices have less than 30 milligrams per 1/2 cup serving: apples, apple juice, apricots, banana, blueberries, cantaloupe, grapes, grapefruit, grapefruit juice, nectarines, orange, orange juice, peaches, pears, pineapple, raspberries, strawberries.

Fish, poultry, meat

FOOD	QUANTITY	PHOSPHOROUS (milligrams)
beef	3 ounces	180
chicken	3 ounces	175

FOOD	QUANTITY	PHOSPHOROUS (milligrams)
eggs	1	100
fish	3 ounces	195
liver	3 ounces	400
salmon	3 ounces	240
tuna	3 ounces	190
turkey	3 ounces	215
Fast foods		
hamburger	1/4 pound	225
pizza	1 slice	170
taco	1	175

Vegetables

Most vegetables have less than 60 milligrams per 1/2 cup serving: asparagus, beans (green), beets, broccoli, brussels sprouts, cabbage, carrots, cauliflower, corn, cucumber, eggplant, lettuce, onions, peppers, potatoes, spinach, summer and winter squash, sweet potatoes and yams, tomatoes, turnips.

FOOD	QUANTITY	PHOSPHOROUS (milligrams)
Legumes have more phosphorous:		
beans: kidney, navy, lima	1/2 cup	140
beans: pinto, garbanzo	1/2 cup	210
lentils:	1/2 cup	120
split peas, black eyed peas	1/2 cup	120
Miscellaneous		
cake with chocolate icing	1 slice	130
chocolate bar	1 ounce	75
nuts	1 ounce (1 tablespoon)	150
peanut butter	1 tablespoon	150

- Many of the foods listed are not recommended for a low cholesterol, low fat, low sodium diet but are included here for your information.

Sources: *Nutrition: The Art of Good Eating.* Seattle, Washington: North West Kidney Foundation, 1989.

Jean A.T. Pennington, Ph.D., R.D., and Helen Nichols Church, B.S. *Bowes and Church's Food Values of Portions Commonly Used,* 1985.

VOLUME AND WEIGHT MEASURES

Volume Measures

1 teaspoon = 1/3 tablespoon = 1/6 fluid ounce = 4.9 milliliters

3 teaspoons = 1 tablespoon = 1/2 fluid ounce = 14.8 milliliters

2 tablespoons = 1/8 cup = 1 fluid ounce = 29.6 milliliters

4 tablespoons = 1/4 cup = 2 fluid ounces = 59.1 milliliters

5-1/3 tablespoons = 1/3 cup = 2-2/3 fluid ounces = 78.9 milliliters

8 tablespoons = 1/2 cup = 4 fluid ounces = 118.3 milliliters

10-2/3 tablespoons = 2/3 cup = 5-1/3 fluid ounces = 157.7 milliliters

12 tablespoons = 3/4 cup = 6 fluid ounces = 177.4 milliliters

14 tablespoons = 7/8 cup = 7 fluid ounces = 207.0 milliliters

16 tablespoons = 1 cup = 8 fluid ounces = 236.6 milliliters

1 milliliter = .034 fluid ounces = 1 cubic centimeter = .001 liter

1 liter = 34 fluid ounces = 1000 milliliters

1 pint = 2 cups = .473 liters = 473 milliliters

1 quart = 2 pints = .9464 liters = 946 milliliters

1 gallon = 4 quarts = 3.785 liters

1 liter = 1.057 quarts = 0.264 gallons = 1000 milliliters

Weight Measures

1 gram = .035 ounces = .001 kilograms = 1000 milligrams = 1,000,000 micrograms

1 milligram = .001 grams = 1000 micrograms

1 ounce = 28.35 grams

1 pound = 16 ounces = 453.59 grams = .454 kilograms

1 kilogram = 2.21 pounds = 1000 grams

Diabetes and Vision Loss Program
of
The Center for the Partially Sighted

Our program will help you to:

- **Improve** blood sugar control and thereby slow the progression of vision loss and other complications;
- **Regain** and maintain independent self-management of your diabetes;
- **Manage** daily activities and move safely about your home and neighborhood.

We achieve these goals by providing **<u>comprehensive low vision care</u>** that may include the following:

- **Optometric Care**-Our doctors enhance your remaining sight to help you perform diabetes-related tasks, like checking your blood sugar levels and taking medication, as well as perform daily living tasks, like paying bills, reading or driving.
- **Rehabilitation Services**-Our instructors teach adaptive strategies that promote independent living, insuring that you are able to self-test and self-medicate, cook, and perform other daily living task and to move about safely in your home and neighborhood.
- **Psychological Services**-Our counselors help people with diabetes gain better control of their blood sugar levels by making changes in glucose testing, diet and exercise as well as helping them cope with the emotional effects of living with a chronic disease.

**For more information, call us at 310-458-3501 X 146
or visit us at www.low-vision.org**

This book made possible by a grant from

MetLife Foundation